CHURCH POLITY

International Studies in Protestant Church Polity

The Journal of the Society
for Protestant Church Polity

INAUGURAL ISSUE

ISSN 2693-2970 (Print)
ISSN 2963-2989 (Online)

Volume 1, Number 1
Winter 2020

Church Polity

Church Polity: International Studies in Protestant Church Polity is a peer-reviewed international journal of church polity from and for the Protestant world. The journal provides a forum for discussion on matters of church polity across denominational and national boundaries. Contributions are welcomed for a variety of approaches that provide for historical, theological, biblical, and legal analyses of church polity topics from around the Protestant world. *Church Polity* originates from the Society for Protestant Church Polity, an international network of church polity scholars and practitioners.

Editors
Klaas-Willem de Jong
Protestant Theological University, Amsterdam/Groningen, The Netherlands
Matthew J van Maastricht
New Brunswick Theological Seminary, New Brunswick, New Jersey, USA

Copy Editor
James Hart Brumm
The Beardslee Press, New Brunswick Theological Seminary, New Brunswick, New Jersey, USA

Layout and Typesetting
Russell Louis Gasero
Wit & Intellect Publishing
Archivist Emeritus, Reformed Church in America

Church Polity (ISSN 2693-2970 (Print); ISSN 2963-2989 (Online)) is published annually by the Society for Protestant Church Polity.

© 2020

ISBN: 978-1-7327952-1-1

Contents

Editorial Introduction

Klaas-Willem de Jong
Matthew J. van Maastricht

Welcome to the inaugural issue of *Church Polity: International Studies in Protestant Church Polity*. This is the scholarly journal of the Society for Protestant Church Polity, an international network of church polity scholars and practitioners in the Protestant traditions.

The Society for Protestant Church Polity began from a conversation between two church polity teachers, Matthew van Maastricht from New Brunswick Theological Seminary (New Jersey, the United States), and Klaas-Willem de Jong from the Protestant Theological University (The Netherlands). We first met at an international church polity conference at Princeton Theological Seminary that was organized by the International Protestant Church Polity Study Group (IPCPSG). The IPCPSG is a loose collective of church polity scholars and practitioners which has sponsored three international conferences (Utrecht, 2011; Pretoria, 2014, and Princeton, 2016) and established begun a book series *Church Polity and Ecumenism: Global Perspectives*, published by LIT. As this conversation progressed, we so greatly appreciated the work of the IPCPSG, and wanted something that would exist as an ongoing network to encourage collaboration and research and to encourage and advance the study of church polity. What began as a conversation, after some time, became a Society with members from five continents who desired a similar network. In fact, many of those involved in the IPCPSG are also involved in this Society.

The world continues to be a place in transition, and the church must respond to the social changes that are happening, globally, with an increasing pace. How is the church to evaluate these changes and what they mean for the church? How does the church respond to these changes? This is exactly the place where church polity scholars and practitioners should be involved. And at the same time that the world is seeing an increasing pace of change, it is not changing in the same way in every place. It was from this desire to learn from other church polity scholars and practitioners from around the world, a desire to build ecumenical and international connections between people to encourage fellowship and scholarship, and to bring renewed attention to the discipline of church polity that this Society was born.

This Society has "Protestant" in the name. As the idea was coalescing, there was a question about the breadth. Since the founders are both from the Reformed tradition, should it be Reformed church polity? Or, on the other side of the spectrum, do we want to be a space for universal church polity/canon law discussion including Roman Catholic canon law or Orthodox canonical tradition? We settled on Protestant not out of a desire to exclude, but rather, to try to find a balance between specificity and diversity and to try to narrow the focus, particularly at the beginning. The Society is focused on the Protestant traditions, but most certainly people from Roman Catholic and Orthodox traditions are able to participate fully in the life and work of the Society.

While different traditions within the Protestant world understand church polity differently, we desired to create a space for this breadth to be present and engage with one another and learn from one another. The Society seeks to be intentionally ecumenical: Reformed, Lutheran, Congregational, Anglican, Methodist, Baptist, Pentecostal, and more. This, in itself, provides for a significant amount of diversity. We desired for a Society to be international, so that we hear the voices not only of different traditions, but also different parts of the world and different national contexts. This greatly enhances the conversation and dialogue and the advancement of the discipline.

An additional goal was to establish a scholarly journal specifically dedicated to church polity in the Protestant traditions. There is research in the discipline of church polity which is published in a host of different journals throughout the world. While affirming the interdisciplinary connections of church polity, we also desired to create a journal dedicated to church polity so that scholars and practitioners around the world might be able to share with others, learn from one another, and to encourage the publication of original research in church polity. Indeed, because church polity intersects with so many other disciplines (e.g. systematic theology, historical theology and church history, law, practical theology, and others), such a journal is naturally interdisciplinary within the primary focus of church polity.

In this first issue, our goal was to provide a broad overview of the current state of Protestant church polity around the world. To that end, we invited a number of scholars from around the world to contribute, and we received acceptances from nearly all of them. This group of scholars represented a good balance of national origin, male and female, global north and global South. As often happens, however, our plans did not finish the way that they were planned. Illnesses and the additional pressures from the COVID-19 pandemic on people working in their respective denominations has meant that the breadth of the essays presented here are not as broad as that for which we had hoped. As such, this issue is the first step in an overview of the state of Protestant church polity around the world, and it is a theme we hope to continue in the next issue, as well.

The content of this issue

We would like to briefly introduce the articles of this issue to you. To begin with, Leo J. Koffeman, emeritus professor and well known for his manual *In Order to Serve*, describes the recent Protestant polity developments in the Netherlands. Godfrey Msiska presents the situation of some Zambian denominations regarding church polity and formulates some solid recommendations for improvement. Indonesian scholar Lazarus H. Purwanto offers an insight in the challenges faced by the Protestant churches in his country in expressing their identity through their church order. Like Msiska, he makes some suggestions to increase the quality of their church polity. Finally, Carlos E. Wilton introduces the current state of affairs of, primarily, the Presbyterian Church (U.S.A.) in the United States.

The four articles are of a very different content and character. Nevertheless, in all four countries and groups of churches described, Protestant church polity is in progress in the last decades. The circumstances and reasons vary. We note a number of remarkably related topics that appear in most, or even all, of the contributions. First, are societal developments, more in particular in the western world secularization. Koffeman sees it as "a multi-layered phenomenon: it contains processes like individualization, privatization, deinstitutionalization, globalization and differentiation."

Second, as a fruit of the ecumenical movement, especially of the establishment of the World Council of Churches in 1948 and its activities thereafter, churches have intensified contacts, sometimes cooperating with each other or even merging. By doing so, churches have been forced to evaluate their present polity as well as the tradition from which they come. Against this background, it is no surprise that the until recently significant role of history and historical sources in church polity has been reduced. While in the past churches put a strong emphasis on mutual differences, in this era of secularization they primarily respond to the call to act and witness together.

Third, these developments cannot be seen in isolation from the third topic we discover; the church is facing huge missionary challenges. Although, from a western perspective people might think this is a typical western theme, the contributions from Indonesia as well as Zambia show it is not. It seems, along with the impact of the ecumenical movement all over the world, a new missionary awareness has come forward. Both developments have influenced each other in a positive way.

Fourth, we see a relationship between the urge to act more missionary and the reflection on the special offices and the office of all the faithful. Though only Msiska and to a lesser extent Purwanto thematize this, their findings may be helpful for western churches struggling with secularization.

Finally, most articles show a direct correlation between social developments, ecclesiastical practice and theological reflection. We value this as a sign of vitality of church polity. Both churches and theologians appear to be able to reflect on and to react to what happens in society and to redefine their positions. The question is, of course, whether they are making the right choices. As founders and present editors of this journal we hope that it will be a forum to question each other critically and, in this way, to improve the quality of the discipline.

Looking Ahead

As was noted above, this is a first step toward a goal of understanding the current state of church polity in the Protestant world. We hope to be able to continue toward a fuller expression of this goal in the second issue. To this end, we welcome additional contributions of this type for the next issue. We wish to present a diversity of voices, churches, contexts, and traditions. This present issue is predominantly Reformed/Presbyterian in orientation, but in keeping with the Society's vision, we particularly invite contributions from the global South and from the diversity of Protestantism. Contributions are welcomed from everyone, member and non-member alike.

Secondly, we would like to ask for other articles on church polity topics. These can come from the perspective of any of the various disciplines that intersect with church polity. While this journal is brand new, we do hope that together we can build its reputation to be a significant voice in the discipline of church polity.

Thirdly, we invite book reviews for recent books published in church polity and church polity adjacent topics. A number of recent volumes have been announced in the Newsletter of the Society over the past year, and any of these, or others, would be excellent for review. If you are in need of a volume to review, please contact us, and we will work to obtain one for you.

And finally, this is the scholarly publication of the Society, we also have a quarterly email newsletter that contains news from and for the Society, including: publication, conference, and employment announcements, personal updates from the Society (awards, fellowships, appointments, and other items of note), and others. Please consider subscribing to the newsletter to keep up to date with the Society. Information about the journal, submission guidelines, the newsletter, and membership in the Society can be found on our website: http://churchpolity.org.

Church Polity In The Netherlands In The Early 21st Century

Leo J. Koffeman

This article describes recent developments in the field of church polity in the Netherlands. A changing ecclesial landscape, due to secularization, has resulted in new legislation. Dutch society now is a post-Christendom society: important areas of public life exist independent of church or religion. Society has lost its common Christian narrative. Church unifications and deregulation are among the main effects in terms of church polity. In 2004, the Protestant Church in the Netherlands was born as a merger of three former churches: new regulations had to be put in place. Several times the new church order was evaluated, leading to steps of deregulation, as e.g. the requirements of the church order for small congregations proved to be too complicated. Cooperation between congregations was made easier, flexibility was favored. A new missionary awareness played a role as well. New forms of church are being developed for people that are not used to going to church. In this context the theological issue of the significance of ministry has come to the forefront. The nominal decrease of Christianity

Leo J. Koffeman is Professor Emeritus of Church Polity and Ecumenism at the Protestant Theological University (Amsterdam) and Extraordinary Professor at the University of Stellenbosch and the University of Pretoria (South Africa).

in the Netherlands has also impacted theological education and research. Staff reductions also had consequences for the time available for theological research in the field of church polity. Nevertheless, new initiatives–a Center for Religion and Law, a journal, an international conference, and several interesting monographs stand out as well. Ecumenical and international cooperation, including theologians as well as lawyers may stimulate research.

In the Netherlands, the first decades of the twenty-first century have seen some interesting and important developments in the field of church polity. This is true for the practical field of a changing ecclesial landscape, resulting in new legislation, as well as for the academic reflection on church polity. I use to circumscribe the theological discipline of church polity as "the systematic analysis, evaluation, and development of the sum total of established rules as a legal system that governs structures and legal relations within churches, as well as their mutual relations and their relations to the respective states, from the perspective of ecclesiology."[1] In this area of theology, church practice and academic reflection are intertwined: academic reflection concerns existing, intended and changing regulations, and practical church order developments reflect changing theological and particularly ecclesiological views.

In this contribution, I want to focus first on some important changes in the field of church life from the perspective of their consequences in terms of church law/order. In a second step, I intend to show what kind of academic reflection has prepared and accompanied such developments. As most articles in this field are written in Dutch, I hope to present some insights that may be interesting for comparison with developments in other parts of the world. This might as well stimulate further international cooperation in this small but vivid part of the academic theological encyclopedia. This will also be the focus of my final, appreciative paragraphs.

Developments in practical church polity

The ecclesial landscape in the Netherlands has seen some major changes over the last decades. They cannot be understood

---

[1]   Leo J. Koffeman, *In Order to Serve: An Ecumenical Introduction to Church Polity* (Zürich: LIT Verlag, 2014), 3.

without a simplified sketch of developments in the wider society. From that perspective, two tendencies stand out.

First, the process of secularization, gaining ever more momentum after World War II, plays a decisive role. Statistics present a clear picture. According to the most recent survey of the *Centraal Bureau voor de Statistiek* (the government office for statistics), less than twenty-four percent of the population identifies itself as Roman Catholic. About fifteen percent is Protestant, five percent is Muslim, and six percent belongs to another religion. Church attendance shows a similar picture. Whereas in 1973 seventy-three percent of the population would attend a worship service at least once a month, the most recent figures say that this number has decreased to about fifteen percent (2017).[2]

Of course, such statistical materials do not tell the whole story. Secularization is a multi-layered phenomenon: it contains processes like individualization, privatization, de-institutionalization, globalization, and differentiation.[3] An important aspect concerns the role of religion in public life. Stefan Paas typifies Dutch society as a post-Christendom society: important areas like science, education, and health care exist independent of church or religion. Society has lost its common Christian narrative.[4] Whereas (explicitly) Christian political parties dominated political life for many decades, with an absolute majority in Parliament until 1967, their number of seats in Parliament is now reduced to about eighteen percent. For the Protestant Church in the Netherlands (PCN), this development towards a post-Christendom society was one of the reasons to reconsider its view on the democratic rule of law.[5]

---

[2]   See Hans Schmeets, *Wie is religieus, en wie niet?* CBS – Statistische trends, 2018, 5-8; other researchers nowadays also suggest that the majority of the population is non-religious.

[3]   Cf. Leon van den Broeke and Eddy van der Borght, "Inleiding," in *Religieus leiderschap in post-christelijk Nederland*, eds. Leon van den Broeke and Eddy van der Borght (Utrecht: KokBoekencentrum, 2020), 9-14, 11.

[4]   See Stefan Paas, "Post-Christian, Post-Christendom, and post-modern Europe: Towards the interaction of missiology and the social sciences," *Mission Studies* 28, no. 1 (January 2011): 3-25. See also Jack Barentsen and Annemarie Foppen, "Post-christendom context in Nederland en België,» in Van den Broeke and Van der Borght *Religieus leiderschap*, 17-36.

[5]   See [Protestantse Kerk in Nederland], De kerk en de democratische rechtsstaat–een positiebepaling. Bijdrage aan het gesprek in gemeente en kerk, [2009], accessed July 16, 2020, www.protestantsekerk.nl/download372.

Second, in this context, the increasing number of Muslims, mainly through immigration, must be noted as well. In terms of figures, a five percent share in the population may not seem to be truly relevant. But it is their attitude towards secularization that confuses many non-religious (and religious) citizens, and that raises suspicion about the compatibility of religion and 'neutral' democracy. Attacks by terrorists who claim to represent Islam have had a major impact on society – and, of course, not only so in the Netherlands. Although about as many Christians immigrated to the Netherlands over the last decades, they are hardly visible in public debate.

In terms of church polity, it is especially secularization that has impacted church legislation and the underlying process of theological reorientation. Basically, we see two developments that are, at least, also influenced by secularization–although it may be too easy to see secularization as the one and only background–i.e. church unification and deregulation.

In 2004, after a process that had lasted for more than 40 years, three churches–the Netherlands Reformed Church, the Reformed Churches in the Netherlands, and the Evangelical Lutheran Church in the Kingdom of the Netherlands–united into the Protestant Church in the Netherlands.[6] Differences that had seemed to be incompatible for decades, could be overcome in a new church order, based on the recognition of the complementarity of the traditionally differing views. These concerned issues like church discipline, plurality, the relation between the local congregation and the national church, and public statements by the church.

A second unification is worth mentioning as well: early 2020, after an exploratory process of a few years, the synods of two smaller churches within the Dutch Reformed family, the Liberated Reformed Churches, and the Dutch Reformed Churches, decided to restore the unity that was broken in the late nineteen sixties.

A second effect of the decrease of church life in terms of membership and participation was the need to deregulate church life, especially in the Protestant Church in the Netherlands. Whereas the new church order of 2004 mainly had the character of a 'unification document,' it soon became clear that in some respects

---

[6]   See Leo J. Koffeman, "How the Protestant Church in the Netherlands was born," in *The Protestant Church in the Netherlands*, eds. Arjan Plaisier and Leo J. Koffeman (Zürich: LIT Verlag, 2014), 11-37.

it was not really helpful for church life in the 21st century. A first evaluation, starting in 2009, of experiences with the new church order already identified several issues that had to be reconsidered. Local congregations, and more particularly the smaller and weaker ones, had major difficulties in meeting the requirements of the church order, for instance with regard to the obligatory minimum size of the local church councils. From 2012, this resulted in a number of church order changes, dealing with the rules for election of office-bearers, the position of church workers, interim-ministers, and many other issues.

In 2016, the general synod launched another process of fundamental re-evaluation of church order procedures and require-ments, under the heading *Kerk 2025* (Church 2025).[7] One of the main principles was 'back to basics.' In order not only to survive but also to be relevant in society, significant changes in the church order were introduced. The quintessence of many of these changes was to make it easier for local congregations to continue with fewer resources in terms of personnel and finances. Tailor-made solutions were made possible, cooperation between congregations was made easier, flexibility was favored. In many cases where, for instance, it had been necessary to ask the classical assembly for permission to act, this rule was cancelled. The supra-local organization of the church, in its presbyteries (classes) and its general synod became slimmer; fewer local office-bearers were needed to constitute these assemblies. New is the possibility to close down a congregation, if–in terms of membership and resources–it is no longer possible to continue its existence.

The introduction of the church order of the PCN, and its later major adaptations, were accompanied by the publication of commentaries, to be used by practitioners like local ministers.[8]

---

[7] See Leo J. Koffeman, "Ordained Ministry: Reformed and Ecumenical Observa-tions," in *Remembrance, Communion, and Hope. Essays in honor of Allan J. Janssen*, ed. Matthew J. van Maastricht, The Historical Series of the Reformed Church in America No 96 (Grand Rapids, MI: Reformed Church Press, 2019), 183-203, 189f

[8] See: P. van den Heuvel, ed. *De toelichting op de kerkorde van de Protestantse Kerk in Nederland* (Zoetermeer: Uitgeverij Boekencentrum, 2004); P. van den Heu-vel, ed. *De toelichting op de kerkorde van de Protestantse Kerk in Nederland – Her-ziene uitgave* (Zoetermeer: Uitgeverij Boekencentrum, 2013); F. Tobias Bos and Leo J. Koffeman, eds. *Nieuwe toelichting op de kerkorde van de Protestantse Kerk in Nederland*. Utrecht: KokBoekencentrum, 2019.

A third, and maybe the most important consequence of the awareness that we live in a secular society is the new missionary attitude of the Protestant Church in the Netherlands – and of many other churches. The traditional form of congregations – although still valuable for many members of the church – does not always seem to appeal sufficiently to the religious and spiritual needs of people in Dutch society, and in various ways congregations have opened themselves to their contexts. New forms of church – like pub churches, and monastic initiatives, including new forms of community life – are developed for people that are not used to going to church. From 2009, the general synod made significant resources available for new missionary projects, new 'church spots' (Dutch: *kerkplekken*), where strongly motivated church members explored new ways of bringing people together around the Gospel. In 2013, the general synod set the goal of a hundred new pioneer spots nationwide. These pioneer spots have become the object of intensive synodical discussion from 2017 and will probably lead to new church order adaptations.

It is in this context of decreasing membership of traditional churches and a new awareness of missionary challenges and op-tions that the theological issue of the significance of ministry has come to the forefront. Still, ministers with an academic theological training are the norm. But in the congregations ever more 'church workers,' with professional training at a less academic level, are being appointed. It is no exception that 'pioneers' have hardly any theological training. This raises the question of what the theological core of ministry is. Which is the value of traditional ecumenical views of ministry, as cherished in the Commission on Faith and Order of the World Council of Churches, in a secularized context? After a decade of intensive discussion, an ecumenical study group including Protestants, Catholics, and e.g. Baptists, recently published a volume on leadership in the Dutch post-Christian context.[9]

Academic church polity

The nominal decrease of Christianity in the Netherlands has also impacted theological education and research. In the second half of the 20th century, ministers for the churches that would later unite

---

[9]   Van den Broeke and Van der Borght, *Religieus leiderschap*.

into the PCN were trained in seven different locations/institutions. Nowadays, they have merged into one Protestant Theological University (PThU), partly operating in cooperation with two other universities in Amsterdam and Groningen. Staff reductions also had consequences for the time available for theological research in the field of church polity. Now, Klaas-Willem de Jong is the only one who teaches church polity, and does research within the framework of PThU, in a part-time position as an Associate Professor. Similar developments affected two other centers of protestant theology,[10] in Kampen and Apeldoorn.[11]

A new institute worth mentioning here is the Centrum voor Religie en Recht (Center for Religion and Law), based in the faculties of law and of theology of the Vrije Universiteit (Amsterdam), under the leadership of Leon van den Broeke. Here, lawyers and theologians cooperate in research in the field of church polity, including issues of constitutional law and civil law like religious freedom or the position of churches in civil law. The Centrum also took responsibility for a journal, *NTKR, Tijdschrift voor Recht en Religie*.[12] In the field of religion and civil law, recently several dissertations were accepted at faculties of law in the Netherlands. At least two of them should be mentioned here. In 2013, P.T. Pel acquired his doctorate with a voluminous study on the legal position of religious ministers in light of the particular status of churches and other religious communities under Dutch law.[13] A few years later,

---

[10] In this article I focus on protestant theology and church polity. However, I want to mention two important recent Dutch publications on Roman Catholic canon law: Ton Meijers, *Compendium van het katholiek canoniek recht. Deel I: Inleiding en volk Gods* (Nijmegen: Valkhof Pers, 2013), and Ton Meijers, *Compendium van het katholiek canoniek recht. Deel II: Verkondiging en sacramenten* (Nijmegen: Valkhof Pers, 2017).

[11] In Apeldoorn Professor Herman Selderhuis has the chair for church history and church polity, but he focuses on church history. In Kampen, Leon van den Broeke is working in a part-time position as Associate Professor for church polity. For his publications see https://research.vu.nl/en/persons/c-van-den-broeke/publications/, accessed July 23, 2020.

[12] See www.uitgeverijparis.nl, accessed July, 17, 2020. In 2019, at the occasion of the 10th anniversary of the journal, a book was published: C. van den Broeke et al., eds., *Perspectieven op de godsdienstvrijheid en de verhouding tussen staat en religie* (Zutphen: Paris, 2019).

[13] P.T. Pel, *Geestelijken in het recht: De rechtspositie van geestelijke functionarissen in het licht van het eigen recht van de kerken en religieuze gemeenschappen in de Nederlandse rechtsorde* (Den Haag: Boom Juridische Uitgevers, 2013).

another civil lawyer, Teunis van Kooten, successfully defended his PhD thesis on the position of churches in Dutch civil law.[14]

A monograph with a theological introduction to church polity, *Het goed recht van de kerk*, was published by the author in 2009.[15] In 2014, LIT Verlag facilitated the publication of an English version of this book, maintaining a similar structure, but including some additional issues and views.[16] It deals with the theological nature of church order as a sub-discipline, in an ecumenical setting, but from the perspective of the Reformed tradition. To what extent is it (still) possible to speak of what has traditionally been understood as 'principles of Re-formed polity'? Are there prescriptions in church order that may be considered essential to the nature of the church? Much of this was based on research during an international study leave and on the input at an international conference in Utrecht on 'Protestant Church Polity in Changing Contexts.'[17] In this conference, in 2011, the PCN cooperated with the PThU in bringing together (mainly Reformed) church polity experts from around the world. The conference was attended by dozens of academics and practitioners, mainly from the Netherlands, the USA, South Africa, and Indonesia, but also from many other countries in Europe, Africa, and Asia.[18]

---

[14]   Teunis van Kooten, *Het kerkgenootschap in de neutrale staat: Een verkenning en analyse van de positie van het kerkgenootschap binnen de Nederlandse rechtsorde* (Den Haag: Boom Juridische Uitgevers, 2017). Cf. also A.H. Santing-Wubs, *Kerken in Geding: De burgerlijke rechter en kerkelijke geschillen* (Den Haag: Boom Juridische Uitgevers, 2002).

[15]   Leo J. Koffeman. *Het goed recht van de kerk: Een theologische inleiding op het kerkrecht* (Kampen: Kok, 2009).

[16]   Koffeman, *In Order to Serve*.

[17]   Many contributions to the conference were published in two volumes: Allan J. Janssen and Leo J. Koffeman, eds. *Protestant Church Polity in Changing Contexts I: Ecclesiological and Historical Contributions. Proceedings of the International Conference, Utrecht, The Netherlands, 7-10 November 2011*. Series: Church Polity and Ecumenism – Global Perspectives 2 (Zürich: LIT Verlag, 2014). Leo J. Koffeman and Johannes Smit, eds. *Protestant Church Polity in Changing Contexts II: Case Studies. Proceedings of the International Conference, Utrecht, The Netherlands, 7-10 November 2011*. Series: Church Polity and Ecumenism – Global Perspectives 3. Zürich: LIT Verlag, 2014.

[18]   A second international conference was held in Pretoria, South Africa, in 2014. Unfortunately, no proceedings were published. The third conference was held at Princeton, New Jersey, USA, in 2016. See: Barry Ensign-George and Hélène Evers, eds. *Church Polity, Mission and Unity: Their Impact in Church Life. Proceedings of the International Conference, Princeton, New Jersey, USA, 18-20 April 2016*. Series: Church Polity and Ecumenism – Global Perspectives 5 (Zürich: LIT Verlag, 2019).

Church polity was dealt with from an historical perspective in a dissertation on the history of the Dordt Church Order (1619), the founding church order for Dutch Protestantism. Dr. Van Harten-Tip meticulously explored the relations between this church order and a number of mainly regional church orders, some of them initiated by civil authorities, that were in use between Emden 1571 and 1619.[19] At two anniversaries a symposium was held, both resulting in smaller booklets with the main lectures. In 2006, it was the 200th anniversary of the *Algemeen Reglement*, the church order introduced by King Willem I in the first years after the birth of the Kingdom of the Netherlands.[20] In 2008, the 100th year of death of F.L. Rutgers, companion of Abraham Kuyper, was commemorated with a symposium on his church polity legacy.[21]

Over the last years, several articles on specific issues in the church order of the PCN were published by Klaas-Willem de Jong, e.g. in *NTKR, Tijdschrift voor Recht en Religie* and in *Kerk en Theologie*.[22]

Perspectives

Church polity has flourished over the last decades, if compared with the situation in, for instance, the second half of the 20th century. At least partly due to secularization, churches had to reconsider their systems of regulations, and academic theologians participated in these discussions – and stimulated them. That is one side of the medal. On the other hand, theological faculties are diminishing in resources, and church polity is not necessarily seen as a core discipline. It is not self-evident that it will survive as a vital theological sub-discipline.

[19]   A. van Harten-Tip. *De Dordtse Kerkorde 1619: Ontwikkeling, context en theologie* (Utrecht: KokBoekencentrum, 2018).

[20]   See Fred van Lieburg, and Joke Roelevink, eds, *Ramp of redding? 200 jaar Algemeen Reglement voor het Bestuur der Hervormde Kerk in het Koninkrijk der Nederlanden 1816-2016* (Utrecht: Boekencentrum, 2018).

[21]   See Leon Van den Broeke and George Harinck, eds, *Nooit meer eene nieuwe hiërarchie: De kerkrechtelijke nalatenschap van F.L. Rutgers.* (Hilversum: De Vuurbaak, 2018).

[22]   A few examples: Klaas-Willem De Jong, "Sacramentsbevoegdheid: van uitzondering naar regel. Pleidooi voor aanpassing van de kerkorde," *Kerk en Theologie* 69 (2018), p. 272-285; Klaas-Willem De Jong, and A.P.D. Zijlstra, "Delegatie? De verhouding tussen kerkenraad en werkgroepen in de kerkorde van de Protestantse Kerk in Nederland," *NTKR Tijdschrift voor Recht en Religie* 2019(-2) [april 2020], 187-204. See further: http://home.planet.nl/~jong9304/home.html, accessed July, 23, 2020.

It is my strong conviction that church polity will only have a future if it, first, intensifies ecumenical cooperation.[23] Second, the cooperation of theologians and lawyers may stimulate research. Third, and most of all, international cooperation will be key to the future of academic church polity. Therefore, this initiative to start a web journal *Church Polity: International Studies in Protestant Church Polity*, has to be welcomed!

---

[23] An interesting project in this respect is initiated by Anglican canon lawyer Norman Doe; see Norman Doe, *Christian Law: Contemporary Principles* (Cambridge: University Press 2013). In 2021 the findings of an international study group under his leadership can be expected: Norman Doe, ed. *Church Laws and Ecumenism: A New Path for Christian Unity* (New York: Routledge 2021).

Church Order and Church Identity Challenges and Opportunities for Churches in Indonesia to Express Their Identity Through Church Order

Lazarus H. Purwanto

Church order is one of the important and fundamental expressions of church identity. However, not all churches in Indonesia understand this well. That is why there is a tendency for the churches to manage matters relating to their church orders in inadequate ways, both theologically and ecclesially. This article presents a theological and ecclesial review and evaluation of the challenges faced by churches in Indonesia in expressing their identity through their church order. This article also offers some steps that can be taken by churches in Indonesia if they are to transform themselves through a church order based on certain church polity principles. In this way it is hoped that the churches in Indonesia will be able to express their identity through church order clearly, completely and effectively.

Introduction

Churches in Indonesia have long been confronted with church order issues. We can observe this mostly in the ecclesial documents,

Lazarus Purwanto is pastor emeritus of the Indonesian Christian Church (Gereja Kristen Indonesia) and part time lecturer at Jakarta Theological Seminary (Sekolah Tinggi Filsafat dan Theologi Jakarta), Indonesia

especially the minutes and/or acts of their synod meetings. In the synod meetings, as shown in these documents, the church order is usually regarded as the main church regulations for dealing with and solving various problems they face. However, sometimes the documents also demonstrate that the church order itself has become a source of problems for the churches in carrying out their ministries. Therefore, a growing number of churches in Indonesia have decided to review and revise their church orders.

The churches exist within the Indonesian national context, which is characterized by huge size and enormous diversity. Situated in Southeast Asia between the Indian and Pacific Oceans with a width of 5,150 kilometers−in the European context, this is equal to the line from Ireland to the Caspian Sea−and with a total number of no less than 17,500 islands, Indonesia is the world's largest archipelago. Indonesia has now around 270 million citizens spreading over more than 3,000 inhabited islands, making it Asia's third and the world's fourth most populous country. There are about 250 ethnic groups, at least twenty-five of which form the major ethnicities, each with a corresponding local language or dialect.

The diversity in terms of religion in Indonesia is also very apparent. There are six world religions−Islam, Catholicism, Protestantism, Hinduism, Buddhism and Confucianism−that are officially recognized in Indonesia. But along with the variety of ethnic groups, there are different religions which have also been accepted and are called traditional faiths (Indonesian: *aliran kepercayaan*). Among all these religions and traditional faiths, Islam−comprising more than 80 percent of the Indonesia −is the biggest.

The churches in Indonesia are also marked by the number and variety of denominations. Currently there are around 27 million Christians (about 10 percent of the population). They belong to more than 350 denominations or church organizations. In terms of church tradition (doctrine/confession and practices), those churches are divided into various streams. Besides the Roman Catholics and the Orthodox (Oriental and Eastern), there are Lutherans, Calvinists, Anglican, Mennonites, Baptists, Methodists, Pentecostal (including Charismatic), Evangelicals, Adventists, Salvation Army, Mormons, Jehovah's Witnesses, Christian Science and New Age Movement.

A number of churches claim themselves to be interdenominational, non-denominational, independent, or ecumenical in character.[1]

Within this context, I have had the opportunity to assist a number of churches in dealing with their church order problems. Since 2009 at least thirteen churches, Calvinist and Lutheran, have invited me to be an expert-consultant on church polity and church order, with varying frequency and intensity. The aim is generally the same, namely to review and revise their church orders which are considered no longer adequate and effective in dealing with and resolving the problems of their lives and ministries.

In addition, my teaching experience on church polity at the Jakarta Theological Seminary (Sekolah Tinggi Filsafat Theologi Jakarta/STFT Jakarta) since 1993 until now has added a relatively wide range of knowledge about the churches in Indonesia. The Jakarta Theological Seminary is the oldest ecumenical theological school in Indonesia. The students come from many different church denominations from all over Indonesia. Through the teaching-learning process, I have gotten to know many church orders in Indonesia. Class discussions have also highlighted the problems of church order faced by the churches. To complete this picture, I have also had the opportunity to gain knowledge and experiences in my own church, Gereja Kristen Indonesia (the Indonesian Christian Church/GKI), as I have been involved continuously as a member of the GKI's Church Order Commission since 1980 until now (only interrupted for several years during my master's and doctoral studies in the Netherlands).

From all of my knowledge and experiences so far, I have come to a conclusion that the main problem faced by the churches in Indonesia is that they have not fully regarded and used the church order as an expression of their identity that underlies and directs

---

[1]   See Jan S. Aritonang, "Current Ecumenical Movement and Spirit in Indonesia" (presentation, the South East Asian consultation on "Churches and Seminaries: Appraising our Ecumenical Vision in Today's World," Manila, the Philippines, November 24-29, 2008). Concerning the Protestant churches in Indonesia, cf. Th. van den End's article, "Denominasi-denominasi Protestan di Indonesia," Koinonia (bulletin of the "Persekutuan Kristen Indonesia se-Eropa"), Easter Edition, 1995, 58-74. According to Van den End, the Protestant churches in Indonesia, from the historical point of view, can be divided into the following denominations: A. Denominations rooted in Europe, namely Calvinist, Uniert (German, "united") and Mennonite; B. Denominations rooted in the U.S.A., that is Methodist, Baptist, "Faith Missions," Pentecostal, Adventist and Salvation Army.

their ministries in their respective contexts. This article is primarily to make a limited theological and ecclesiastical review and evaluation of the struggles and challenges faced by the churches. I am convinced that every church in Indonesia must develop and transform its church order as an expression of its identity based on contextual ecclesiology and in accordance with appropriate and relevant church polity principles.

Given the limited space in this article, not all aspects related to church order will be discussed. In this article we will only deal with some aspects of church order that are considered fundamental.

Ecclesiological Basis

Church order is based on ecclesiology. A church order is always built on a foundation in the form of a certain ecclesiology.[2] What

---

[2]   W. Bakker states that "Het kerkrecht wortelt in ecclesiologie, de leer aangaande de kerk" ("The church polity is rooted in ecclesiology, that is the teachings about the church") (W. Bakker, "Wat is kerkrecht?" In *Inleiding tot de studie van het kerkrecht*, W. van 't Spijker and LC van Drimmelen, eds., [Kampen: JH Kok, n.d., 13]). G.D.J. Dingemans argues further that "Een kerkorde is gestructureerde en in praktijk gebrachte theologie. Of nog preciezer gezegd: een kerkorde is een in rechtsregels vertaalde ecclesiologie" ("A church order is a theology that is structured and brought into practice. Or, if more precisely expressed: a church order is ecclesiology translated into regulations") (Dingemans, "Kerkorde als ecclesiologische vormgeving," in *Inleiding tot de studie van het kerkrecht*, 207). Leo J. Koffeman, who was my main promoter in my doctoral study, has already explained the ecclesiological approach at a glance in his book, *Gestalte en gehalte: Oecumenisch-theologische en kerkrechtelijke implicaties van het visitekaartje van de VPKN* (Kampen: THUK, 1994, 4-5). Koffeman then develops the ecclesiological approach by providing a basic and complete theoretical framework, using an ecumenical lens and in a global perspective, in a textbook of church polity, *In Order to Serve: An Ecumenical Introduction to Church Polity* (Zurich and Münster: LIT Verlag, 2014). The more classical books in the field of church polity, written by Pieter Coertzen, namely *Church and Order: A Reformed Perspective* (Leuven: Uitgeverij Peeters, 1998) and *Decently and In Order: A Theological Reflection on the Order for, and the Order in, the Church* (Leuven: Uitgeverij Peeters, 2004), do not specifically mention the ecclesiological approach. However, in these books it is clear that Coertzen develops the principles of church polity from certain ecclesiological grounds. I myself have started to use the ecclesiological approach in an initial, simple way in the study of church polity in my master's thesis, "Towards the Church Polity with the Indonesian Perspective: A Critical Analysis of the Church Order of the Central Java Indonesian Christian Church" (The Theological University of the Reformed Churches in the Netherlands, Kampen, The Netherlands, 1990, unpublished). I then develop this approach further in my dissertation at the same theological university, *Indonesian Church Orders under Scrutiny: The Relationship between the Church Members and the Church Office-Bearers - How It Is and How It Should Be* (Kampen: Drukkerij Van Den Berg, 1997).

is meant by ecclesiology here, roughly defined, is the theological-systematic formulation of the church's understanding of itself. In the ecclesial realm, it can also be regarded as an expression of the church's confession of faith regarding "the Church."

It goes without saying that if a church intends to develop its church order, first of all it must outline its ecclesiological design. In this regard, it must be noted that there is no such thing as *the* ecclesiology. Every church in its historical context must have its own ecclesiology in different forms of explicit and formal formulae. Considering the relation between church order and ecclesiology as mentioned above, the basic formulations of ecclesiology must be explicitly set out in and become the foundational part of the church order. I suggest that the foundational ecclesiological ideas are placed in the preamble of the church order.

Almost all church orders in Indonesia begin with a preamble (Indonesian: *pembukaan* or *mukadimah*). However, the preamble usually does not contain actual ecclesiological ideas as the foundation of the church order. In general, the preamble of the existing church order is more focused on the historical background of the church and its legal status. This is in fact understandable because there are no churches in Indonesia which purposely use an ecclesiological approach in developing the church order. The approach that has usually been used by churches in developing their church order is what I call the church government system approach. For example, a Calvinist church will naturally regard a presbyterial-synodal system as the basis and main reference for developing its church order.[3] In my opinion, this particular way of thinking and working in dealing with church order is neither appropriate nor adequate, because the life and ministry of the church basically is not determined by the system of church government. I always propose that this approach be abandoned and replaced with an ecclesiological approach.

At the initial meetings with the churches, I usually facilitate the discussions to critically review and evaluate the preamble of the existing church order before determining the subsequent steps. Right from the start I suggest that the church adopt an ecclesiological approach in developing or revising its church order. By using this particular approach, the church will develop by itself

---

[3]   In view of the many church traditions and denominational streams in Indonesia, I plainly take this just as an example.

the basic ecclesiological ideas which in broad outline address the relationships and tensions between:

- The universal nature of the church, both from a biblical perspective[4] and ecumenical view.[5]
- The nature and mission of the church in particular (synodal/denominational), in its general, historical, cultural and contemporary multi-contexts.[6]
- The nature and mission of the local church.

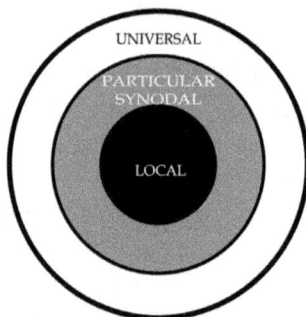

Figure 1

[4] Biblically, with a trinitarian lens, the church is understood and recognized as the "Church of the Triune God," through the images of "People of God," "Body of Christ" and "Temple of the Holy Spirit." This is expressed explicitly in the ecumenical document on ecclesiology currently issued by the World Council of Churches (WCC), *The Church: Towards A Common Vision* (hereinafter referred to as *The Church*) (Geneva: WCC Publications, Faith and Order Paper No 214, 2013, §13-21).

[5] Ecumenically, the main reference is undoubtedly the confession of faith concerning the church in the Nicene-Constantinopolitan Creed, that the church is "One, Holy, Catholic and Apostolic" (see *The Church*, §22-24; cf. WCC, *Confessing the One Faith: An Ecumenical Explication of the Apostolic Faith as it is Confessed in the Nicene-Constantinopolitan Creed (381)* [Geneva: WCC Publications, Faith and Order Paper No 153, New Revised Version, 1991], 81-90). In developing the church polity principles, Koffeman has used the *Una Sancta* as a basic reference (*proprietates* or attributes of the church) for arranging the quality markers of the church (*In Order to Serve*, 131-233) as ecumenical church polity principles.

[6] The cultural background, ideas and practices of a particular church within the context of enormous cultural diversity in Indonesia is definitely a very important layer here. A cultural field research to explore the sources of church identity as raw material for developing a contextual ecclesiology for Gereja Masehi Injili di Timor (the Christian Evangelical Church in Timor/GMIT) can be put forward as an excellent example: J. Campbell-Nelson, "Sumber-sumber Identitas Gereja: Bahan Baku Eklesiologi Kontekstual," in *Seputar Teologi Operatif*, B.A. Abednego, ed. (Yogyakarta: Penerbit Kanisius, and Jakarta: BPK Gunung Mulia, 1994), 53-85.

As I have already mentioned above, the basic ecclesiological ideas should be formulated and stated in full in the preamble of the church order. In this way, the identity of the church will be presented ecclesiologically through the church order.

Self-Definition

Generally speaking, church orders in Indonesia include in their first articles the identity of the church concerned in the form of regulations. These articles usually focus on the name of the church, place and time as the spatial and temporal aspects of the church as an institution, as well as the legal status of the church. It can be presumed that this kind of regulatory model follows the statutes of Indonesian social institutions. With this model, the church, perhaps unintentionally, identifies itself more as an ordinary social institution. In that way the church has apparently lost the opportunity to define itself as the church based primarily on ecclesiological ideas and church polity principles.

That is why I always suggest that the first articles of the church order be filled with basic regulations that contain the full, complete and schematic self-definition of the church. Such self-definition is of great importance because in general the existing church orders contain self-definition of the church that is not well formulated, spread out sporadically, and in formulations that tend to be ambiguous or multi-interpretative. For this reason, I offer a scheme for formulating the church's self-definition as follows:

Name of ecclesial scope	Form of community	Leadership institution/ board	Church meeting
Congregation			
Classis/presbytery or equivalent			
Regional synod or equivalent			
Synod			

Figure 2

In practice the formulating process is by no means simple. Along with following the above scheme, the church simultaneously has to pay attention to and comply with four basic ecclesiological aspects that a church's self-definition has to have (see "Ecclesiological Basis" above), as illustrated below:

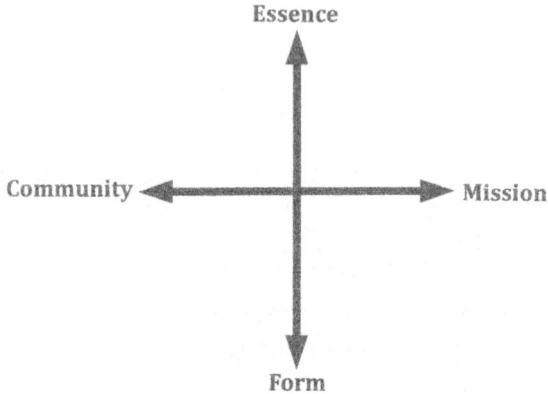

Essence

Community ←————————————→ Mission

Form

Figure 3

Following these guidelines altogether, every part of the scheme as shown in Figure 2 has to be defined one by one respectively in deliberate, accurate and consistent manners.

Self-definition of the church that has been formulated schematically, integrally and completely at the beginning of the church order will then be the main and basic reference for formulating all regulations in other parts of the church order. In this way, all the regulations in the church order as the comprehensive church's self-definition—thus as the whole church identity—can be formulated schematically, consistently and effectively.

Congregation as Basic Community

What is the basic community of the church (see Figure 1)? In my observation, this fundamental question was apparently not given serious thought when the church formulated its existing church order. There seems to be a general tendency in the church orders that the synod is regarded as the "basic" form of community that underlies the existence and mission of the church as a whole. This is quite evident in the formulation of sporadic regulations, especially concerning leadership institutions. Generally, the chain of leadership institutions starts from the synodal leadership body which then "goes down" to other leadership institutions that are placed under it. In this way, we can see and find in the church order a model or structure of ecclesial community that is oriented toward the synod–being a kind of synodalism–which tends to be hierarchical and centralized in character.

Therefore I suggest and encourage churches in Indonesia to regard and place the congregation as the basic community of the church (see again Figure 1) for at least two reasons. Empirically, the congregation as a social system in the society is the most concrete and living community. In my experience, this is indisputable. But this social premise alone is not enough as this is only one side of the coin. Essentially, the congregation is a community of faith, whose basic meaning is explicitly stated ecclesiologically in *The Church*:

> The local church [congregation] is a community of bap-
> tized believers in which the word of God is preached, the
> apostolic faith confessed, the sacraments are celebrated, the
> redemptive work of Christ for the world is witnessed to, and
> a ministry of *episkopé* exercised by bishops or other ministers
> in serving the community.
>
> Each local church contains within it the fullness of what
> it is to be the Church. It is wholly Church, ... [though it is] not
> the whole Church.[7]

By positioning the congregation as the basic community of the church, the communities that are formed in other ecclesial scopes, namely classis, regional synod, and synod (see Figure 2), are regarded and placed as the extensions of the congregation. As such, all forms of community in the church are qualitatively equal and stay on one and the same level with no communal hierarchy whatsoever (see Organizational Structure below). The formulations of the manifested, not necessarily concrete, forms of the church's community listed in the second column of Figure 2 are based on this church polity principle.

Mission

In general, the churches in Indonesia provide mission a prominent place in the church order and formulate the mission of the church as a major part of it. If we briefly compare the formulations of the mission of the church, it can be seen that the churches understand and formulate their mission as a threefold mission, that

[7]   WCC, *The Church*, §31.

is *koinonia* (Indonesian: *persekutuan*), *diakonia* (Indonesian: *pelayanan*) and *martyria* (Indonesian: *kesaksian*). Apparently this particular threefold mission scheme has been accepted and followed by the churches for a long time, becoming an ecclesial tradition that tends not to be critically reviewed.[8] Unfortunately I have not found a historical-missiological study in Indonesia that addresses this topic in depth and comprehensively.

In each meeting I attended as consultant, I always suggested and encouraged the churches to conduct some theological-ecclesiastical study to review and formulate their mission in an open and contextual manner. Given the limited nature of the meetings I attended, there was usually no opportunity to discuss a critical review of the understanding of the church mission completely.

I then usually offer an alternative to the missional ideas developed by the World Council of Churches.[9] This idea can be called a three-dimensional mission of the church. In the basic view that the church is *koinonia*, the mission of the church has three dimensions that cannot be separated from one another. This special missional idea can be described as follows:

The church as *koinonia*	
Dimension	**Expression**
Faith dimension of koinonia Character: Vertical	Living in communion with Triune God
Life dimension of koinonia Character: Horizontal-internal/centripetal	Sharing a common life in Christ
Witness dimension of koinonia Character: Horizontal-external/centrifugal	Witnessing for a renewed world

Figure 4

8   This view has generally been followed by the Communion of Churches in Indonesia (Persekutuan Gereja-gereja di Indonesia/PGI) (formerly the Council of Churches in Indonesia [Dewan Gereja-gereja di Indonesia/DGI]) and its member churches since the 1970s (see my survey and conclusions in my dissertation: *Indonesian Church Orders under Scrutiny*, 162-195, especially 193-195).

9   See the official report of the Fifth World Conference on Faith and Order, published in the book *On the Way to Fuller Koinonia*, edited by Thomas Best and Gunther Gassman (Geneva: WCC Publications, Faith and Order Paper No. 166, 1994). I also used the WCC scheme as the framework for developing basic ecclesiological ideas in my dissertation (*Indonesian Church Orders under Scrutiny*, 157-161).

By presenting this idea, I hope that the churches will receive and be able to learn from an ecumenical understanding of the church mission. I believe that this could be an important part in the formulating processes of the church mission in their church orders.

One more thing has to be put forward here. As said above, the synod is commonly regarded as the basic form of community that underlies the existence and mission of the church. Consequently, the church mission is formulated as the synodal church mission. This cannot be left without change. With reference to Figure 2 and Figure 3, the mission of the church must be formulated as the mission carried out by the church in all its forms of community, with the congregation as the basic community. In other words, the missional identity of the church must start with and be developed from the congregation as the church's basic community.

Membership

In the church orders in Indonesia, church membership is generally regulated in terms of the categories of membership as well as its rights and responsibilities. Based on baptism, membership consists of two categories of members, namely the baptized member (that is those who have received infant baptism; Indonesian: *anggota baptisan*) and the confessing or confirmed member (that is those who have received adult baptism or baptized members who have made a profession of faith; Indonesian: *anggota dewasa* or *anggota sidi*). In some churches, there is one additional category, namely the member who is automatically registered based on her/his birth in a Christian family who are already members. In this case, there are regulations that are mixed and ambiguous between membership based on baptism and membership based on birth.

If the church is a fellowship of baptized persons, it is very clear that the ecclesiological basis of church membership is the sacrament of baptism, no matter whether it is adult baptism or infant baptism. This theological principle is stated explicitly in the World Council of Churches's (WCC's) document, *Baptism, Eucharist and Ministry* (hereinafter referred to as *BEM*):

> Baptism is the sign of new life through Jesus Christ. It unites the one baptized with Christ and with his people.[10]

---

[10] "Baptism," WCC, *BEM*, §2.

Administered in obedience to our Lord, baptism is a sign and seal of our common discipleship. Through baptism, Christians are brought into union with Christ, with each other and with the Church of every time and place. Our common baptism, which unites us to Christ in faith, is thus a basic bond of unity.[11]

Thus, the regulations on church membership in church orders must only refer and adhere to this ecclesiological basis. As Hans Küng emphasizes, baptism is "the entry into the community."[12] The principle of membership based on birth may have certain historical backgrounds so that it is traditionally accepted by some churches in Indonesia without question. This requires further historical research. However, I am of the opinion that church membership based on birth has no ecclesiological foundation and cannot be maintained any longer.

Arrangements regarding the rights and obligations of church members presumably show that the church views itself as an ordinary social organization. In social organizations in Indonesia, membership is usually understood primarily from the aspects of rights and obligations, prioritizing the rights of members. If this is the case, provisions like this must be revised and replaced by baptism-based membership regulations. From this perspective we can affirm that baptism is not only the entry into the community, but also "the entry into the ministry."[13] This is stated clearly in *BEM*:

When baptismal unity is realized in the one holy, catholic, apostolic Church, a genuine Christian witness can be made to the healing and reconciling love of of God.[14]

It [baptism] gives participation in the community of the Holy Spirit. It is a sign of the Kingdom of God and the life of the world to come. Through the gifts of faith, hope and love, baptism has a dynamic which embraces the whole life, extends to all nations, and anticipates the day when every tongue will confess that Jesus Christ is Lord to the glory of God the Father.[15]

[11]   "Baptism," WCC, BEM, §6.
[12]   Hans Küng, *The Church* (Garden City, NY: Image Books, 1976), 273; cf. Purwanto, *Indonesian Church Orders under Scrutiny*, 301-303.
[13]   Purwanto, *Indonesian Church Orders under Scrutiny*, 302-303.
[14]   "Baptism," WCC, BEM, §6.
[15]   "Baptism," WCC, BEM, §7.

Following this line, what is regulated in the membership section undoubtedly is not the rights and obligations of members as in social organizations. What should primarily be addressed at this point is the missional calling of the church members to carry out their Christian ministries comprehensively in their lives. In this way, this section will connect church membership with the mission of the church, because it is the church members who are the main actors/subjects who carry out the church's mission. At the same time, this section also relates the church's mission to the world where the church's mission is to be realized. It is here that we definitely find the most concrete and operational manifestation of the church's identity, that is the ministries of church members in everyday life in the world as the accomplishment of the mission of the church.

Church Office

All church orders have an appropriate section for the regulations of church offices. However, if we read them carefully from the perspective of church polity, we will come to the conclusion that the regulations regarding church offices are generally inadequate. Some church orders regulate church offices in a sketchy way as if they were not an important subject matter for the church and subsequently for the church order. There are church orders that only mention the categories of church offices in detail but do not describe their main ecclesial functions. There is even a church order that only mentions one church office explicitly, namely the pastor (Indonesian: *pendeta*). In that particular church order there are actually other categories of church offices, but they are inappropriately and ambiguously identified as "church council" (Indonesian: *majelis jemaat*).[16] There are even some church orders in which the pastor as an ordained ministry is regarded and regulated as an "employee" (Indonesian: *karyawan* or *pegawai*) of the church.

On various occasions, I have always emphasized that it is not enough that the church order provides a section to regulate church offices. From ecclesiological and church polity principles, the church offices must be regulated in the church order in a basic, complete and functional way that is at the same time rooted in a

---

[16]   Church council cannot be categorized as a church office at all because, although its members are church office-holders, it is itself a collective ecclesial institution or board.

theology of ministry. Ecclesiologically, church offices are essential and constitutive for the life and ministry of the church. This is decisively stated in *BEM*:

> In order to fulfil its mission, the Church needs persons who are publicly and continually responsible for pointing to its fundamental dependence on Jesus Christ, and thereby provide, within a multiplicity of gifts, a focus of its unity. The ministry of such persons, who since very early times have been ordained, is constitutive for the life and witness of the Church.[17]

In this ecclesiological line, *The Church* confirms that in the historical and eschatological journey of the churches in the world as communion (*koinonia*) in their unity and diversity, the church office–together with the apostolic faith and the sacraments–is identified as an essential element:

> The journey towards the full realization of God's gift of communion requires Christian communities to agree about the fundamental aspects of the life of the Church. "The ecclesial elements required for full communion within a visibly united church –the goal of the ecumenical movement– are communion in the fullness of apostolic faith; in sacramental life; in a truly one and mutually recognized ministry; in structures of conciliar relations and decision-making; and in common witness and service in the world." These attributes serve as a necessary framework for maintaining unity in legitimate diversity.[18]

Regarding the essential nature of the church office, *BEM* outlines further the main functions of the church office, as follows:

> The chief responsibility of the ordained ministry is to assemble and build up the body of Christ by proclaiming and teaching the Word of God, by celebrating the sacraments, and by guiding the life of the community in its worship, its mission and its caring ministry.[19]

---

[17]   "Ministry," WCC, *BEM*, §8.
[18]   WCC, *The Church*, §37.
[19]   "Ministry," WCC, *BEM*, §13.

By holding on to the essential, ecumenical understanding of church office above, every church must contextually develop its own regulations on church offices in an adequate and comprehensive way. The section on church office in the church order must consist at least of two substantial aspects. First, it must present pointedly the categories of church offices, and second, it must describe in detail the main functions of every church office for the life and ministry of the church. The identity of the church expressed through the church order depends proportionally on the ecclesiological understanding of the church offices and their subsequent ecclesial functions.

In this regard, the churches in Indonesia are faced with a very difficult question: do they accept and practice a hierarchy of church offices, ecclesiologically and ecclesiastically? Whatever ecclesiological and ecclesiastical stand is taken, the church should develop either non-hierarchical or hierarchical church offices in the church order that are explicitly based on sound and comprehensive ecclesiological, historical and contextual foundations.

Another serious theological problem is also faced by churches in Indonesia that have views, explicitly or implicitly expressed and regulated, that the pastor is the church's employee. From common ecclesiological grounds and church polity principles, it is totally clear that the views and regulations regarding the pastor as the church's employee are diametrically opposed to the nature and function of the pastor as church office. In this case the churches concerned have to make radical changes, fundamentally and totally rethinking these views and regulations. In practice, to change a long-standing ecclesiastical tradition as this one is by no means easy. However, if the church wants to be true to its nature and wants to reveal its identity as the church of the Triune God, such changes are inevitable and urgent.

Organizational Structure

The church's organizational structure on the bottom line is about the basic and operational relations between the church as a community of people and the church office-bearers as leaders of the people, both personally and collectively.[20] Churches in Indonesia,

---

[20] This is the main theme of my research in my dissertation, *Indonesian Church Orders under Scrutiny*. Koffeman, in *In Order to Serve*, with a liturgical church polity frame, places the relationship and tension between "the congregation" and "ordained ministry" as the foundation and nature of the church (Koffe-

as demonstrated by their church orders, do not have the same or uniform organizational structures. This is understandable. This article in fact does not intend to make any generalization about the matter. However, in general it can be asserted that there is a certain tendency in view of how the churches develop their organizational structure.

Commonly speaking, church orders in Indonesia give considerable attention and extensive place for regulating ecclesial organizational structures. It is no exaggeration to say that sometimes the church order can be called a "structure order." This does not rule out the fact that the church orders usually contain ambiguous and inconsistent regulations concerning the church structures. I've also observed that they are rarely presented in an adequate, systematic way.

Along with the tendency of the churches to regard the synod as the basic community form in their ecclesial existence as a whole (becoming a sort of synodalistic model of community), in the church orders the synodal leadership institution also tends to be placed and arranged to become the center and at the same time the top or "crown" of the ecclesial organizational structures (see Figure 2). As already mentioned above, it goes without saying that this synodalistic model makes the congregations only as part of the synod.

To explain further this particular church structure, let us pay attention to the figures below. In the perspective from above, if the church synodal community is connected with the synodal leadership institution—usually called the synodal council (Indonesian: *majelis sinode*)—we will get a centralistic structural design as in Figure 5.

If we place the same relationship between the church synodal community and the synodal leadership institution in a three-dimensional perspective, we will see a hierarchical pyramidal design like in figure 6:[21]

Considering the reality of such church orders, I usually suggest and urge the churches to develop their church structures based on the church's self-definition by using the instrument in

---

man, *In Order to Serve*, 83-128). For a general understanding of organizational structures see, among others, J. Hendriks *Een vitale en aantrekkelijke gemeente: Model en methode van gemeenteopbouw* (Kampen: Uitgeverij Kok, 1990), 76-77; cf. Mady A. Thung, *The Precarious Organisation: Sociological Explorations of the Church's Mission and Structure* (s-Gravenhage: Mouton & Co., 1976), 209.

[21]   In this way the two designs in Figure 5 and Figure 6 are complementary.

**Centralistic church structure
(perspective from above)**

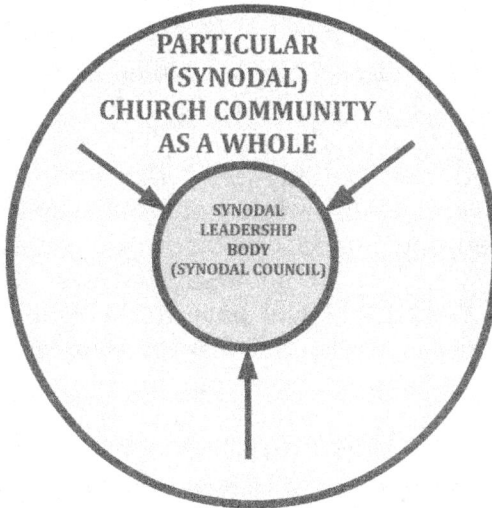

Figure 5

**Hierarchical church structure
(three-dimensional perspective)**

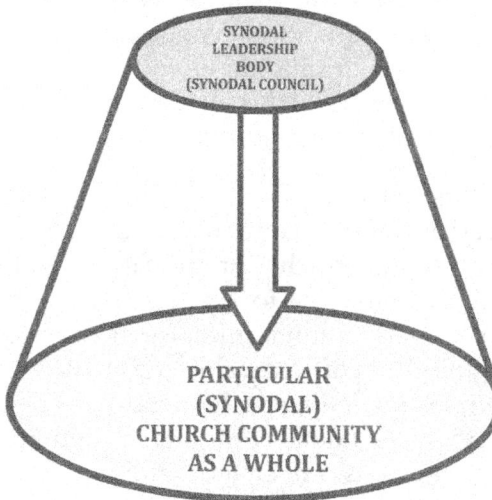

Figure 6

Figure 2. Basically, church structure must be built and developed as an inseparable part of the church's self-definition. In other words, the church structure is an important part of expressing the identity of the church.

For this fundamental reason, I then openly and strongly challenge the churches to regard and position the congregation as *the* basic community of the church. I emphasize firmly that the view of the synod as the basic community of the church does not have any ecclesiological foundation and cannot be explained sociologically either. This inappropriate ecclesiological and ecclesiastical notion should be abandoned. This is not to say, however, that the synodal community is denied and will have to be removed. Using the instrument in Figure 2 it is clear that the synodal community–as an integral part of the church's community as a whole–can be regarded and placed proportionally and logically as the widest ecclesial community of the church. The forms of other internal communities will then be arranged sequentially according to the basic organizational system of church order of the particular church. All these structural arrangements will finally actualize the life of the church as a whole, intact community, as stated in *The Church*:

> Under the guidance of the Holy Spirit, the whole Church is synodal/conciliar, at all levels of ecclesial life: local, regional and universal. The quality of synodality or conciliarity reflects the mystery of the trinitarian life of God, and the structures of the Church express this quality so as to actualize the community's life as a communion.[22]

Some points have to be put forward here. It must be emphasized that in church community forms, there is no such thing as a communal hierarchy. Empirically it is not possible for a wider ecclesial community to be regarded as if it is "above" other narrower ecclesial communities. In other words, all forms of ecclesial community of a particular church always stand on one-and-the-same level ground. Following the scheme in Figure 2, synodal community, regional-synodal community (and its equivalents), and community of classis/presbytery (and its equivalents) cannot be seen as "supra-congregational" communities. The determinative

---

[22] WCC, *The Church*, §13.

point of departure in this method of "expanding community forms" is the congregation as the church's basic community form. With this method the whole communal identity of the church through the church order can be developed properly.

Then, following the scheme in Figure 2 and based on the communal structure that has been defined, the relationships between the ecclesial leadership institutions of the respective community forms can be subsequently arranged. The method I recommend is what I call the method of "establishing an equal network of leadership institutions."[23] This method is used with the assumption that the church has established the principle of ecclesiological and ecclesiatical equality for its church offices. If the church has ecclesiologically and ecclesiatically decided to establish a hierarchical structure among its church offices, which is legitimate, then the decision will become the logical starting point for the construction of hierarchical ecclesial leadership structures. This is not discussed in this article.

Building equal leadership networks rests on the leadership authority in the leadership institutions. The leadership authority is also referred to as the authority to carry out the ministry of oversight (*episkopé*).[24] Given the limitations of this article, here we will only briefly describe three principles. The first principle is the biblical basis. *The Church* explains biblically that ecclesiastical authority is rooted in the Triune God, which at the same time is understood as originating from Jesus Christ as Head of the Church:

> All authority in the Church comes from her Lord and head, Jesus Christ, whose authority, conveyed with the word *exousia* (power, delegated authority, moral authority, influence; literally "from out of one's being") in the New Testament [...].[25]
>
> Thus, authority in the Church in its various forms and levels, must be distinguished from mere power. This authority comes from God the Father through the Son in the power of the Holy Spirit; as such it reflects the holiness of God.[26]

---

[23] Cf. the concept of "shared leadership" developed by Ford (*Transforming Church*, 127-161).

[24] WCC, *The Church*, §48.

[25] WCC, *The Church*, §48.

[26] WCC, *The Church*, §50.

From here, the ecclesiastical authority is stated as having the basic character of love and is not a dominating or coercive one:

> Thus, the Church's authority is different from that of the world. When the disciples sought to exercise power over one another, Jesus corrected them, saying that he came not to be served but to serve, and to offer his life for others (cf. Mark 10:41-45; Luke 22:25). Authority within the Church must be understood as humble service, nourishing and building up the *koinonia* of the Church in faith, life and witness; it is exemplified in Jesus' action of washing the feet of the disciples (cf. John 13:1-17). It is a service (*diakonia*) of love, without any domination or coercion.[27]

The second principle is that the network of ecclesial leadership authority must be established by departing from the congregation as the basic community of the church (see again above parts).

> Jesus' entire ministry was characterized by authority (Mark 1:27; Luke 4:36) which placed itself at the service of human beings. Having received "all authority in heaven and on earth" (Matt. 28:18), Jesus shared his authority with the apostles (cf. John 20:22). Their successors in the ministry of oversight (*episkopê*) exercised authority in the proclamation of the Gospel, in the celebration of the sacraments, particularly the eucharist, and in the pastoral guidance of believers.[28]

In this way, the synodal leadership institution (read: synodal council) is purposely not placed in the middle as the center or positioned above in a hierarchical structure of all leadership bodies in the church. It is positioned as one of the many, but with specific ecclesial functions.

The third principle is related to the functions of the leadership institutions as a whole in the network that is being built. This principle follows the premise "form follows function." It can be said briefly here that the functions have two directions that are to be taken simultaneously. On the one point, the functions of all leadership institutions are focused on the congregation as the basic community so that the congregation as a local representation of the

---

[27]   WCC, *The Church*, §49.
[28]   WCC, *The Church*, §48.

church can fully and effectively express its missional identity in its particular context. In this direction, the functions of all the broader leadership institutions are to support, equip and strengthen the congregations.

> In every case *episkopé* is in the service of maintaining continuity in apostolic faith and unity of life. In addition to preaching the Word and celebrating the Sacraments, a principal purpose of this ministry is faithfully to safeguard and hand on revealed truth, to hold the local congregations in communion, to give mutual support and to lead in witnessing to the Gospel. Such guidance includes the oversight of the various Christian service organizations dedicated to bettering human life and to the relief of suffering, aspects of the Church's service (*diakonia*) to the world [...].[29]

On the other point, following the scheme in Figure 2, all the broader leadership institutions at the same time carry out their leadership functions in their respective ecclesial communities. If all of these can be developed and formulated properly with a systemic approach, the identity of the church as a whole will be complete and intact.

Church Transformation

From the perspective of church polity, the church expresses its identity through church order. In the realm of the concrete life of the church, church order is one of the church's tools for realizing the church's ministries. Thus, as an important "service tool" (Indonesian: *alat pelayanan*), so to say, the church order is indispensable for the life and witness of the church in the world. But in Indonesia there has been a fairly broad trend that church order is regarded as the main reference in the churches' life and ministry. This tendency can lead the churches to have a legalistic attitude towards the church order. In this tendency a church order's regulations are viewed, interpreted and accomplished using an interpretive framework of positive law. In my opinion, such views and practices must be abandoned. The church order is important, but it must be placed and used proportionally for the life and witness of the church. It has utterly to be proportional because the church order is not everything for the church.

---

[29]   WCC, *The Church*, §52.

If the church wants to show a total and dynamic life and wants to realize its missional calling in the world as fully and effectively as possible, the church must undergo continuous transformation. In these processes of transformation, "the church as it exists" (the church's *das Sein*) is deliberately pursued to become the "church that it should be" (the church's *das Sollen*). What needs to be emphasized here is that church order does not play a direct and operational role in the efforts to transform the church. Generally speaking, these transformation efforts occur in what in the academic tradition in the Netherlands is called congregational development (Dutch: *gemeenteopbouw*)[30] or what in the academic tradition in the United States is called church revitalization or congregational studies (or the like).[31]

Basically, given the importance and breadth of its scope, the subject matter of church transformation must be discussed separately. Suffice it here to bring forward two important things related to the theme of this article. First, regarding the transformation itself. Kevin G. Ford, in his book *Transforming Church: Bringing Out the Good to Get the Great*, mentions correctly that what is called the real transforming change is not sanitary or tidy (in fact, it's messy, complex, maddening, multidimensional, uncertain, elusive, and often dirty), it cannot be dictated, it is not momentary or temporary, and it is not linear and sometimes even unpredictable.[32]

The second thing that needs to be said is the complexity of the transformation of the church as an institution or organization. In this case we can learn from Francis J. Gouillart and James N. Kelly through their book, *Transforming the Organization*.[33] The

[30]   Just to give an idea, some classic books on *gemeenteopbouw* can be mentioned here: G.L. Goedhart, *Gemeenteopbouw: Om dienende, vierende, lerende en dienende gemeente te worden* (Kampen: J.H. Kok, 1984); R. Bons-Storm, *Geloof waardig: Stappen op de weg van gemeenteopbow* ('s-Gravenhage: Boekencentrum, 1987); J. Hendriks, *Een vitale en aantrekkelijke gemeente: Model en methode van gemeenteopbouw*; and J. Hendriks, *Terug naar de kern: Vernieuwing van de gemeente en de rol van de kerkeraad* (Kampen: J.H. Kok, 1995).

[31]   Some books can be given here just as examples: James F. Hopewell, *Congregation: Stories and Structures* (Philadelphia: Fortress Press, 1987); Nancy T. Ammerman, Jackson W. Carroll, et al., eds., *Studying Congregations: A New Handbook* (Nashville: Abingdon Press, 1998); Diana Butler Bass, *The Practicing Congregation: Imagining A New Old Church* (Herndon, Va.: The Alban Institute, 2004); Kevin G. Ford, *Transforming Church: Bringing Out the Good to Get the Great* (Colorado Springs: David C. Cook, 2008).

[32]   Ford, *Transforming Church*, 201-217.

[33]   Francis J. Gouillart and James N. Kelly, *Transforming the Organization* (New York: McGraw-Hill, 1995).

book was written specifically for business enterprises using a biological and systemic approach. Gouillart and Kelly define the transformation of business organizations as "the orchestrated redesign of the genetic architecture of the corporation, achieved by working simultaneously—although at different speed—along the four dimensions of Reframing, Restructuring, Revitalization and Renewal."[34]

Regarding the four-dimensional scheme of organizational transformation, Gouillart and Kelly explain,[35] that:

- Reframing is the shifting of the company's conception of what it is and what it can achieve.
- Restructuring is a demand for the corporate loins, getting it to achieve a competitive performance.
- Revitalization is about igniting growth by linking the corporate body to the environment.
- Renewal deals with the people side of transformation, and with the spirit of the company.

The church is absolutely not a business organization and definitely cannot be regarded as one. However, by learning from Gouillart and Kelly, it is hoped that the church can carry out transformation processes for itself more effectively in the dimensions of reframing, restructuring, revitalization and renewal. Indeed in this regard the church must also learn from other theories of organizational transformation. The decisive point is that in the overall knowledge and efforts of church transformation, the church order has a proportionally important and indispensable role. What is meant here is this: the church order must be able to provide comprehensive and strong bases in the ecclesiological, structural, and missional-ministerial aspects for church transformation.[36] In

---

[34] Gouillart and Kelly, *Transforming the Organization*, 7.

[35] Gouillart and Kelly, *Transforming the Organization*, 6-8.

[36] To my knowledge, the Indonesian Christian Church might become the first Protestant church in Indonesia to use the paradigmatic transformation of the church in its church order. In the Church Order of GKI 2003 (*Tata Gereja GKI* [Jakarta: Badan Pekerja Majelis Sinode GKI, 2003]) and the Church Order of GKI 2009 (*Tata Gereja dan Tata Laksana GKI* [Jakarta: Badan Pekerja Majelis Sinode GKI, 2009) the idea of church transformation has been expressed ecclesiologically in the Preamble and in the sections concerning membership, church office, and leadership institutions. There is even a special section in both church orders that contains general guidance on how the transformation of the church is to be carried out in the congregation.

negative terms, the possibility that the church order's regulations in practice become obstacles or even hindrances for the church transformation efforts must be avoided. Positively, we must state that the church order has to be intensively and continuously oriented to the transformation of the church for the sake of its open and functioning identity in the world.

Epilogue

The challenges faced by the churches in Indonesia in expressing their missional identity through their church orders are very real and urgent. These challenges should not be left unchecked, but must be answered by every church by making efforts to transform its church order fundamentally and thoroughly using the right church polity method and principles. Three notes need to be put forward to close this article.

First, in light of the churches' leadership structures that are generally centralized, the synodal leadership institutions should have sensitivity enough to the urgent need to make changes to the church order. Following this, naturally it is the synodal leadership institution that is supposed to take the first initiative to facilitate the transforming changes of church order. Their total commitment is also needed so that the processes of change of the church order can be well designed and implemented.

Second, churches that intend to change their church orders need to prepare the plan of change sufficiently far in advance. In my experiences, the church often do not consider the importance of determining the duration for the church order change processes, as if it can be done in a short time. In my opinion, generally speaking the churches in Indonesia must provide at least two years to realize this purpose.

Last but not least, changes to church order require resource persons who have adequate knowledge and abilities in the field of church polity and church order. The churches in Indonesia generally have experts in various fields of theological study and ecclesial ministry. However, the handling of church order issues so far has clearly indicated the lack of human resources in the area of church polity and church order. To overcome this, there are at least two things that should be of concern to the churches. First, the churches need to encourage and send their pastors who have a remarkable interest in church polity and church order to pursue further studies in theological schools that provide church polity studies.[37] Second, interchurch ecumenical openness and cooperation is needed for the churches to help one another in overcoming this problem.[38] If this is done, the churches in Indonesia will be able to move forward together ecumenically in order to become more effective in expressing their missional identity and presence on the beloved Indonesian soil.

[37] It can be stated hypothetically here that the lack of pastors/theologians in the churches in Indonesia who have pursued and mastered the studies of church polity and church order correlates considerably with how theological schools in Indonesia provide the field of church polity studies in their curricula. This remains to be proven in comprehensive research. It is sufficient now to note that making such research concerning theological schools in Indonesia is not easy. In the midst of the number and diversity of denominations (read: the synods) of churches in Indonesia as stated above, there are no less than 380 theological schools of various streams of church tradition, of unequal size and academic quality, which are spread throughout Indonesia. Among them there are currently only fifty-seven theological schools registered with Persetia (Perhimpunan Sekolah-sekolah Teologi di Indonesia/Association of Theological Schools in Indonesia). The challenges of conducting such research are even greater if we realize how many of them provide websites with complete information that is easily accessed by the public.

[38] In this connection it should be noted that the Jakarta Theological Seminary where I teach has so far produced seven masters of theology in church polity from various churches in Indonesia. In addition, two doctors of theology in the field of church polity have been graduated from the seminary, both of them are female theologians: Rev. Dr. Vera Loupatty from Gereja Masehi Injili di Minahasa (the Christian Evangelical Church in Minahasa/GMIM) who is now a lecturer at Fakultas Teologi Universitas Kristen Indonesia di Tomohon (Theological Faculty of Indonesian Christian University in Tomohon/UKIT, Tomohon, North Sulawesi) and Rev. Dr. Jusni Herlina Saragih from Gereja Kristen Protestan Simalungun (the Simalungun Protestant Christian Church/GKPS, North Sumatra) who is now a researcher at the GKPS Synod Office (in Pematangsiantar, North Sumatra). It is hoped that they all can become resource persons in the field of church polity and church order, not only in their respective churches, but also in neighboring churches that need assistance and training for developing or revising their church orders.

A Survey of Developments in Presbyterian Church (USA) Polity in the Past Twenty-Five Years

Carlos E. Wilton

Since denominational reunion in 1983, the polity of the Presbyterian Church (USA) has become simpler and more flexible, in service to denominational peace and to the need of church councils (sessions, presbyteries, synods and General Assembly) to become more innovative in mission.

Polity

Although "polity" is a term scarcely used outside the church setting, everyone instantly recognizes its close linguistic cousin, "politics." Both are descended from the same Greek word: *polis*, meaning "city" or "community." Ecclesiastical polity and secular politics are merely the means by which communities govern themselves.

The likely reason we talk of polity in the church—rather than politics—is that church folk cringe at the word. Conventional wisdom declares that, beyond the stained glass, politics brings

Carlos E. Wilton is transitional pastor of the First Presbyterian Church of Hawley, Pennsylvania and an adjunct professor at Princeton Theological Seminary, teaching Presbyterian polity and worship.

division: so, well-meaning church members urge their pastors to "keep politics out of the pulpit." The word carries connotations of unsavory tactics: the proverbial stomach-turning glimpse of sausage being made. The phrase "church politics" is nearly always pejorative: a derisive jab at conduct the speaker views as something less than Christian.

It need not be so. Politics, according to the word's historic meaning, was not a dirty business. We can see this in a less-common word: "impolitic." A person described as impolitic is violating peaceful norms. Within that uncommon word hides a kinder, gentler vision of politics: a concept dating back to the Greek philosophers, indicating voluntary submission to rules that lead to good results: mutual cooperation, a free exchange of ideas, a healthy airing of grievances and — ultimately — a peaceful, unifying outcome.

Call it polity or politics, the true goal of such service to the *polis* is peace.

Presbyterian Polity: Increasingly Flexible

In the past twenty-five years or so, Presbyterian Church (USA) polity has been becoming more flexible, in service to peace. Two factors in particular have driven this change: (1) the forty-year conflict in the denomination over ordination standards relating to those in same-sex relationships and (2) a growing awareness that, with the gradual demise of the unofficial establishment of mainline Protestantism in the United States, presbyteries and congregations need freedom to innovate as they re-invent their mission.

Before considering the most significant developments in Presbyterian polity in this period, it may be helpful to spend a few moments describing the distinctive features of Presbyterian polity for those not so familiar with it.

Presbyterianism — as the name suggests — is centered around the presbytery: that mid-level institution of governance, composed of two types of members: ministers and congregations. A clear indication that the presbytery is the center of presbyterian governance is found in Volume Two of the PC(USA) Constitution, the *Book of Order*, which states that "Powers not mentioned in this Constitution are reserved to the presbyteries" (G-3.0101).[1] This

---

[1]   *The Constitution of the Presbyterian Church (USA), Part II: The Book of Order, 2019-2021* (Louisville: Office of the General Assembly), 2019.

is the ecclesiastical equivalent of the Tenth Amendment to the US Constitution that declares: "The powers not delegated to the United States by the Constitution, nor prohibited by it to the states, are reserved to the states respectively, or to the people."

The primacy of the presbytery is likewise seen in the terminology the *Book of Order* uses to describe the rare procedure by which a presbytery may remove the session (elected governing board) of a troubled congregation, replacing it with a special commission: that move is called "assuming original jurisdiction" (G-3.0303e). Clearly, jurisdiction is vested in the regional, not the local, level.

Just as, in the Roman Catholic Church, jurisdiction belongs to the bishop and is delegated to parish priests, in the Presbyterian system jurisdiction belongs to the presbytery and is delegated by that body to local sessions. In the unhappy event that a congregation closes its doors and disperses, ownership of its real estate – which the congregation has long held in trust for the presbytery – reverts to the parent body.

It is often said that presbyterian governance is "connectional," as opposed to "congregational" or "episcopal." In a purely congregational polity, congregations are independent units that voluntarily choose to associate with other congregations. In episcopal polity, a single individual, the bishop (*episkopos*, in the Greek) has ultimate oversight of everything that takes place in a congregation.

Presbyterian connectionalism is intended to be a bridge between these two systems, a middle way. In presbyterianism, the role of the bishop is divided. Presbyteries, as a legislative assembly, function as a corporate bishop with respect to governance. Ministers of the Word and Sacrament function as liturgical bishops as they exercise the foundational episcopal roles of preaching and presiding at the Lord's Table.

Everyone voting at a presbytery meeting must be a presbyter (*presbuteros* or "elder," in the Greek) – ordinarily, either a minister or a ruling elder elected as a commissioner.[2] Great care is taken to

---

[2] Alternatively, some ruling elders may be credentialed *ex officio* by virtue of some other role they play in governance: "Ruling elders elected as officers of the presbytery shall be enrolled as members during the period of their service. A presbytery may enroll, or may provide by its own rule for the enrollment of, ruling elders during terms of elected service to the presbytery or its congregations" (G-3.0301).

insure that the overall numbers of each type of presbyter are as equal as possible.

The first type of presbyter, ministers of the Word and Sacrament, are alternatively named teaching elders (G-2.0501). They are not members of congregations, but are individually members of the presbytery. The second type are ruling elders (G-2.0301). They remain members of their congregations, even as they serve as commissioners to their presbytery or to higher councils of the church.

The Constitution of the Presbyterian Church (USA) is divided into two volumes: *The Book of Confessions* and the *Book of Order.* The Book of Confessions is a collection of twelve historic confessional statements, from the Nicene Creed to the PC(USA)'s Brief Statement of Faith (1990).[3] Collectively, these documents form the theological foundation of the church's life and ministry. The *Book of Order,* principally concerned with polity, is comprised of four parts: the Foundational section (general principles), the Form of Government (specific guidance for governance), the Directory for Worship (specific guidance for the conduct of worship) and the Rules of Discipline (procedures for adjudicating conflict).

Evolution from Prescriptive to Descriptive Polity

Experts in the field of English grammar tend to sort themselves into one of two opposing camps: the prescriptivists and the descriptivists.

Grammarians of a prescriptivist bent see themselves as experts in rules that govern the most felicitous use of the language. For them, the rules of grammar are first principles, strictly followed and rarely changed.

Descriptivists, on the other hand, view language as more malleable. To them, grammatical rules and dictionary definitions are snapshots of common language usage at a particular point in time. Language is constantly evolving, so grammar handbooks and dictionaries are always a work in progress, based on collected observations from published sources that reveal how English-speaking populations around the world are actually using the language. For descriptivists, today's irregularity may become tomorrow's best practice, or at least an acceptable alternative.

---

[3]   *The Constitution of the Presbyterian Church (USA), Part 1: The Book of Confessions* (Louisville: Office of the General Assembly), 2016.

The most contentious debates in the field of English—such as the use of the Oxford comma, the suggestion that two spaces must follow a period and the use of "they" as a singular, gender-neutral pronoun—often find expression in either prescriptivist or descriptivist terms.

In reality, it is more accurate to view the prescriptivist/descriptivist divide less as a battle between entrenched factions and more as positions along a spectrum. The two perspectives complement one another, with grammarians demonstrating varying degrees of preference for one position or the other. In reality, even the most ardent prescriptivist accepts the reality that language changes over time, and the most determined descriptivist appreciates the usefulness of standards.

Something similar is at work when it comes to polity. To the extent that polity changes—and, for the PC(USA), every biennial General Assembly offers the opportunity to approve constitutional amendments for ratification by a majority of the presbyteries—there will always be some who prefer a complex *Book of Order* with regulations that anticipate every conceivable situation that may arise. At the same time there are other Presbyterians—a bit more comfortable with coloring outside the lines—who prefer a lean, flexible document that is strong on general principles but flexible enough in its specifics to allow for local differences.

The story of the past twenty-five years in PC(USA) polity is that of a continuous movement away from polity prescriptivism towards a more descriptivist perspective. Within the *Book of Order*, the two most significant developments have been completely new editions of the Form of Government (2011) and the Directory for Worship (2016), resulting in significantly shorter, less detailed documents.

A Brief Glimpse at the Presbyterian Polity Family Tree

Although its roots date back to the earliest days of European settlement in North America, the current form of the Presbyterian Church (USA) came into being in 1983, with the reunion of the United Presbyterian Church in the USA (UPCUSA) and the Presbyterian Church in the US (PCUS).

The PCUS, with congregations located mostly in the southern states, was formed in a Civil-War-era schism as a pro-slavery denomination in the Confederate States of America. At the time of reunion, it remained an almost exclusively southern denomination.

The UPCUSA at that time had congregations throughout the country, although most of its southern congregations were historically black churches.

The UPCUSA had itself been formed in 1958 as a reunion of what was then known as the Presbyterian Church USA and the United Presbyterian Church of North America (UPCNA) — a denomination with roots in the Scottish Covenant and Seceder tradition. The PCUS had been in negotiation with the other two Presbyterian denominations in what was envisioned to be a three-way merger, but the plan foundered when a majority of PCUS presbyteries voted against it. The PCUSA and the UPCNA did indeed merge, forming the United Presbyterian Church in the USA, but it would take a generation for the third partner in the proposed merger to find its way in, as the PCUS finally did in 1983. Even then, a notable minority of conservative PCUS churches broke away to form the Presbyterian Church in America.

One feature that eased the 1983 merger was the fact that the respective polities of the UPCUSA and the PCUS had remained remarkably similar over more than a century of separate existence. A few divergences did emerge, primarily having to do with the nomenclature, examination, and ordination of ministers. When the two tectonic plates of the antecedent denominations gently collided, a few tremors were felt that continued to resonate years later — and, to a lesser degree, continue to do so today.

Polity Developments Following Reunion

Although a 25-year historical survey would ordinarily begin in 1995, the impact of the 1983 reunion is such that it makes sense to tack another dozen years onto the period we are examining.

At the time of the 1983 reunion, both denominations relied on constitutional documents as polity sourcebooks: the UPCUSA version being called the *Book of Order* and the PCUS version the *Book of Church Order*. In addition, since 1967 the UPCUSA had utilized a *Book of Confessions* as a first volume of its Constitution: a collection of historical confessions. Prior to that time, the UPCUSA had relied solely on the *Westminster Confession* and its associated catechisms, as did the PCUS: until 1977, when it supplemented the Westminster documents with a brief confession of its own, *A Declaration of Faith*.[4]

---

[4]   Available online at: https://www.presbyterianmission.org/resource/declaration-faith/

The *Book of Confessions* adopted by the new denomination in 1983 was that of the UPCUSA. It included the Westminster documents, along with the *Apostles' and Nicene Creeds, The Scots Confession* (1560), the *Heidelberg Catechism* (1563) and the *Second Helvetic Confession* (1561). It included two twentieth-century confessions as well: the *Theological Declaration of Barmen* (1934) and the UPCUSA's *Confession of 1967*. The PCUS' 1977 *Declaration of Faith* was never formally added to the Constitution, although in 1985 the General Assembly commended it as a resource for study and teaching.

In later years, two more confessional documents were added to the book: the 1990 *Brief Statement of Faith*, and, in 2016, the *Belhar Confession* from South Africa. Currently under consideration is a proposal to add Martin Luther King, Jr.'s *Letter from Birmingham Jail*.

Anyone examining the pre-reunion *Book of Order* and *Book of Church Order* side by side will immediately be struck by the difference in size. The UPCUSA *Book of Order* visibly takes up more shelf space than the spare PCUS equivalent. In addition, the UPCUSA Office of the General Assembly published—and annually revised—two other books that could be described as Presbyterian midrash: *Presbyterian Law for the Local Church* and *Presbyterian Law for Presbytery and Synod.*[5] These are detailed commentaries on the UPCUSA *Book of Order*.

The comparatively larger size of the UPCUSA *Book of Order*—a feature that continued in the *Book of Order* of the new denomination as well—was the result of a gradual trend that had been going on for decades. Most of this growth took place during the 18-year period beginning in 1966, when William P. Thompson began serving as Stated Clerk of the General Assembly. Thompson led the UPCUSA through a period of centralization of administrative authority at both the General Assembly level and at the level of synods (regional groupings of presbyteries). In 1972, under his leadership, the church's system of smaller, mostly statewide synods was consolidated into large regional groupings. During this period, nearly every presbytery in the country retained—in addition to its

---

[5]   Eugene Carson Blake, ed., 1981 revision by William P. Thompson, *Presbyterian Law for the Local Church* (New York: Office of the General Assembly), 1981. William P. Thompson, ed., *Presbyterian Law for Presbytery and Synod* (New York: Office of the General Assembly), 1973.

elected moderator, stated clerk, and treasurer—the services of at least one full-time executive presbyter. In some parts of the country, those executives were considered to be staff members of the new regional synods, their work coordinated by a synod executive.

Thompson, a ruling elder, was an attorney, and did not consider detailed legal language as anything to be feared. The *Book of Order's* burgeoning verbiage—the greatest growth being focused in the chapter having to do with ministry—meant that a detailed knowledge of the text (not to mention facility at navigating its extensive index) was essential. Seminary polity classes came to resemble law-school courses.

The period after the 1983 reunion was characterized by many adjustments, seeking to reconcile the two streams of tradition. The two books of order were eventually consolidated into one. The ensuing years brought a number of overtures to the General Assembly from presbyteries seeking to restore familiar practices that had been left out of the new book.

Most of these overtures had to do with ministry. Prior to reunion, the UPCUSA and the PCUS had developed different practices connected with the location of examination and ordination for ministers of the Word and Sacrament. In the UPCUSA these most often took place in the presbytery of care: the presbytery in which the candidate's home church was located. In the PCUS, it was the presbytery of call—the location of the new work—that conducted the ordination. Over the next several years, amendments shifted the locus of examination and ordination back and forth between the presbytery of call and the presbytery of care (although always with the option of the two presbyteries agreeing to a different arrangement). It has settled out, at last, with the presbytery of call being the ordinary locus of examination and ordination (G-2.0702).

In the case of already-ordained ministers receiving a new call to a different presbytery, the PCUS practice had always been to have the presbytery of call conduct a theological examination of its member-elect. UPCUSA presbyteries, by contrast, did not examine ministers transferring in from another presbytery at all; the only time a minister was examined on the floor of presbytery was at the time of ordination. The PCUS practice prevailed in the PC(USA) *Book of Order,* although former UPCUSA presbyteries, to this day, are not generally noted for the rigor with which they conduct such examinations.

The years following reunion were characterized by growing theological conflict related to the ordination of sexual minorities, particularly gay, lesbian, transgendered, and queer people. Both denominations, at the time of reunion, prohibited such ordinations, but each year successive overtures arrived at the General Assembly requesting a change. Many of these battles were fought in the form of constitutional amendments to the chapter dealing with qualifications for ministerial ordination, although in later years the section of the Directory for Worship dealing with marriage also became a polity battleground. Eventually, the denomination settled for a position tolerant of local variations in practice.[6] Local presbyteries (and sessions, in the case of deacons and elders) have freedom to make their own decisions on a case-by-case basis, but effectively the denomination as a whole has become LGBTQ-friendly.

The decades-long debate over LGBTQ ordination — that began in the UPCUSA with the General Assembly's first pronouncement on the subject in 1976 — resulted in finely-tuned procedures for Authoritative Interpretations of the Constitution (known as AIs for short).[7] While the General Assembly always reserved the right to issue constitutional interpretations, this practice became increasingly common as the ordination debate raged on. Over time, a successive series of AIs gradually loosened the top-down strictures on the ordination of sexual minorities, allowing ordaining bodies (presbyteries and sessions) greater flexibility to make decisions on the ground. The long-lasting impact of this process has been that the right of ordaining bodies to make their own decisions has been strengthened.

Binding constitutional interpretations come from two different sources: the General Assembly itself, in the form of AIs, and from the Assembly's Permanent Judicial Commission (PJC) in the form of judicial rulings. The Office of the General Assembly has collected many of these interpretations in the _Annotated Book of_

---

[6]   W-4.0601 now describes marriage as "a unique commitment between two people" rather than "between a man and a woman."

[7]   Among the powers of the General Assembly described in G-3.0501c is "authoritatively interpreting the most recent edition of the _Book of Order_ in a manner binding on the whole church, in accordance with the provisions of G-6.02 or through a decision of the General Assembly Permanent Judicial Commission in a remedial or disciplinary case, with the most recent interpretation of the _Book of Order_ being binding."

Order, an online resource offering detailed footnotes to individual paragraphs of the *Book of Order*.[8] The *Annotated Book* is a polity wonk's playground.

With respect to the Rules of Discipline — that fourth part of the *Book of Order* that guides Presbyterians in pursuing remedial and disciplinary cases through the church's judicial system — recent years have brought an increasing focus on non-judicial methods of resolving conflict. The cost of judicial process — financially as well as in human terms — is immense. The *Rules of Discipline* now make room for alternative forms of resolution (or AFRs) that utilize methods such as mediation to avoid courtroom-style proceedings (D-2.0103). Both parties in a remedial or disciplinary case must consent to pursue an AFR, which offers the reward of a more amicable resolution of the problem. Should the AFR fail, resuming the ordinary disciplinary process is still an option.

A New *Form of Government*

Although the Thompson-era predilection for a highly-detailed *Book of Order* prevailed in the years immediately following reunion, a yearning arose for a simpler book that allowed more room for flexible decisions at the local level. In part, this was a result of the bruising debates over sexual ethics — in which "local option" offered the promise of resolving some of the toughest conflicts — but it also reflected a growing realization that the church needed greater flexibility to order its mission and ministry in a rapidly-changing world.

In 2011, after years of labor by a special working group, the General Assembly received the approval of a majority of the presbyteries for a new Form of Government. Acronym-loving Presbyterians immediately labeled it "nFOG." A tremendous amount of detail was removed from the book, particularly from the chapter dealing with ministerial order. Sessions, presbyteries, and synods were urged to craft local policies that filled in the blanks, recording them in newly-mandated manuals of administrative operations (G-3.0106).

The prior Form of Government had specified numerous variants of congregational ministry positions — among them stated supply, designated pastor, interim pastor, and temporary supply.

---

[8]   Available at: http://oga.pcusa.org/section/mid-council-ministries/constitutional-services/constitution/.

In the case of some parish-ministry variants, there were detailed constitutional provisions concerning movement from one category to another, even to the point of specifying what percentage of vote was required for a presbytery to authorize an exception. All these positions became subsumed under a new, inclusive category of temporary pastoral relationships (G-2.0504b). Presbyteries are still free to use the old categories, but are no longer required to do so.

The old book had included a requirement that sessions manage a list of inactive church members, and offered detailed instructions for how a person got onto or off the inactive roll. That requirement disappeared completely in the new book (G-1.04). Again, the emphasis was on local option: sessions could choose to use or not use an inactive roll as a tool for pastoral care.

Perhaps the most controversial change in the 2011 Form of Government had to do with the nomenclature of the orders of ministry now known as ministers and ruling elders. In the pre-1983 antecedent denominations there had been two different systems of nomenclature for presbyters. Prior to reunion, the elder/minister pairing was preferred in UPCUSA churches. An alternate formulation, whose heritage lay principally with the PCUS, was to name these two orders teaching elders and ruling elders.

The post-1983 *Book of Order* named the minister/elder pairing as primary, while noting that these two orders could alternatively be called teaching and ruling elders. In the ensuing years, former PCUS presbyteries presented a succession of overtures asking for a change from "minister" to "teaching elder," none of which received approval from the General Assembly. "Teaching elder" proponents were well-represented on the working group drafting the new Form of Government, and consequently their proposal flipped the order, naming the teaching elder/ruling elder pairing as primary and the minister/elder pairing as secondary.

Because the entire text of the new Form of Government—shorter than its predecessor, but still lengthy—was presented on the floor of the General Assembly as a single motion, there was little opportunity for debating or amending specific changes in wording. The teaching elder/ruling elder nomenclature emerged intact, even though a majority of the church—not to mention ecumenical partners—were more familiar with "minister" than the somewhat obscure "teaching elder."

In 2016, after growing discomfort with the "teaching elder" nomenclature, the General Assembly approved — and a majority of presbyteries concurred with — a change back to the prior practice of treating "Minister of the Word and Sacrament" as the primary title and "teaching elder" as secondary (G-2.0501). In practice, a majority of the denomination — outside of formal meetings of presbyteries, synods, and the General Assembly — had never made the change to begin with.

Other nomenclature changes arrived with the 2011 Form of Government that were less controversial. The generic name for elected decision-making bodies originally known as "courts," later "judicatories," and — in the pre-2011 Form of Government — "governing bodies" became "councils." Councils of the church include sessions, presbyteries, synods, and the General Assembly — but, significantly, not congregations. Congregations are, in and of themselves, "not sufficient to be the church." The work of elected councils who "nurture, guide, and govern those who witness" is also necessary (G-3.0101).

Another change was to replace the title "Commissioned Lay Pastor" with "Ruling Elder Commissioned to Particular Pastoral Service": an unwieldy formulation that has since been shortened, in practice, to the less-descriptive but more prosaic "Commissioned Ruling Elder" (G-2.10).

The 2011 book removed all occurrences of "office" describing ordained positions. Instead of speaking of "offices" of ministry, the preferred term is now "ordered ministry" (G-2.0102). This is in order to distinguish the functional Presbyterian theology of ministry from the official concept prominent in the Roman Catholic and Episcopal traditions.

The Debate Over Synods

Another feature of this period was a protracted debate over the future of synods — that council of the church located between presbyteries and the General Assembly. Historically, synods have organized and overseen the work of presbyteries and are themselves overseen by the General Assembly (G-3.04).

Beginning in the 1990s, voices began to be raised in many parts of the church, questioning whether synods are truly necessary in a time of rapid travel and instantaneous communication. Presbyteries already had the ability to convey actions directly to the General Assembly in the form of officially-enacted overtures, bypassing their synods. Increasing financial pressures led many Presbyterians to wonder whether simply eliminating that level of governance altogether—along with the resulting financial savings—would streamline the church's mission.

In 2010, a new section, "Reduced Function," was added to the section of Chapter 3 describing the work of synods (G-3.0404). This allows a two-thirds majority of the presbyteries in a synod to declare their synod to be a reduced-function synod. Practically speaking, such a move reduces the functions of the synod to two: the review of presbytery minutes and the maintenance of a permanent judicial commission to hear disciplinary cases—primarily appeals sent up from the presbytery level. The elected assembly of a reduced-function synod meets as seldom as every two years and typically employs a minimal staff.

At the present time, there are a variety of patterns around the country with respect to the way synods operate. Some have reduced their functions and others have not. In some parts of the country, as presbyteries—faced with dwindling financial resources—have themselves had to reduce staff and programming, there has been a new appreciation of the value of synods to accomplish certain kinds of work in a centralized and more affordable manner. The future of synods in the PC(USA) is still evolving.

A New *Directory for Worship*

In 1988, the UPCUSA approved a new and greatly expanded Directory for Worship, that was paired with an extensively-revised *Book of Common Worship*. Ever since 1637, when an irate worshiper named Jenny Geddes memorably flung a prayer stool at the head of a minister in Edinburgh's St. Giles' Cathedral after he tried to introduce an Anglican-style *Book of Common Prayer*, Presbyterians have a long and fraught history with service books. Generally, the solution has been to include general guidance for conducting worship in constitutional documents, while making prayer books optional. Some have described the role of these resources as comparable to a map and compass: the map being the optional service book and the compass being the Directory for Worship.

Both the 1988 Directory for Worship and the 1993 *Book of Common Worship* received great acclaim, but — consistent with the desire for a more simplified, tightly-organized document to match the simplified Form of Government, as well as to address some additional questions that had arisen — in 2016 the General Assembly approved, and the presbyteries subsequently adopted, a new, simplified Directory for Worship. A revised and expanded *Book of Common Worship* followed, with updated prayers and worship materials.[9]

Additional Developments

Space does not allow us to address further developments in polity, but here is a listing of some other significant actions taken during the period we have been considering:

1996–The General Assembly rejected an overture to create a list of "essential tenets" of the faith to use in examining candidates for ordination. A similar proposal was rejected again in 2014.

1998–The General Assembly approved a collection of modern-day catechisms and commended them to the church for use in teaching and worship.[10]

1998–The General Assembly approved a revised translation of the Nicene Creed for the *Book of Confessions*.

1998–The General Assembly approved a Formula of Agreement for orderly transfer of ministers among the PC(USA) and the Evangelical Lutheran Church in America, the Reformed Church in America, and the United Church of Christ.[11] In 2008, similar agreements were crafted with the Korean Presbyterian Church in America and the Moravian Church.[12]

2004–The General Assembly gave governing bodies (now called councils) permission to conduct voting by email, as

---

[9]   Office of Theology and Worship for the Presbyterian Church (USA), *Book of Common Worship* (Louisville: Westminster John Knox), 2018.

[10] Presbyterian Church (USA), *Book of Catechisms: Reference Edition* (Louisville: Geneva Press, 2001).

[11] Appendix B to the *Book of Order*.

[12] The agreement with the KPCA is found in Appendix C of the *Book of Order*, and with the Moravian Church at: https://www.pcusa.org/site_media/media/uploads/oga/pdf/moravian-pres-cov.pdf.

long as provision is made for deliberation using simultaneous communication and such vote is provided for in standing rules.

2014–A majority of presbyteries approved including a new translation of the Heidelberg Catechism in the *Book of Confessions*.

An Examination of Church Members' Perceptions of Church Orders in Zambia: Towards a More Sustainable and Inclusive Church Polity Strategy

Godfrey Msiska

This article explores the church members' perceptions of church orders in Zambia from the church historical perspective. Drawing on church polity and church history in discussing the contemporary situation of Zambia, thus the article discusses the church members' perceptions of church order and its polity, the demand for competence of church leaders in interpretation of church orders, availability of trained church leaders in church polity, commitment of church policy makers, and competence of church members for implementation of church orders. It concludes with observations about the need to strengthen both church order and church polity.

Introduction

In Zambia, like in most other countries of the world, a church order is developed to serve the mission of a particular denomination. Church order, according to Pieter Coertzen, should be made for a

---

Godfrey Msiska is a PhD Student at University of Pretoria and a Minister in the Uniting Presbyterian Church in Southern Africa. He is also lecturer and Head of School of Theology at Evangelical University in Zambia.

particular church and for a particular time. Church order has broad goals to help in the governance of a denomination.[1]

Church polity has a long tradition of helping many denominations to achieve theological objectives, through theological education obtained from either churches or theological institutions. Church polity in Zambia began along with the European missionaries with the aid of a British colonial government, and during the colonial era it gained ground. After Zambia gained political independence, Zambia's theological education grew quite rapidly due to the fact that the education which was offered to the Africans started making people more aware of taking initiative in theological education. However, European missionaries delayed ministerial training for Africans, and this delayed ministerial training affected the involvement of competent church leaders in leading churches after political independence in Zambia. It was after 1965 when the churches in Zambia moved away from the former practice of the European missionaries of delayed training of Africans for leadership.

The church orders in Zambia appear both non-directional and irrelevant to the needs of both the church and its church members. Although churches in Zambia are committed to implementing its church orders and its polity, this theological education in church polity appears to fall short of requirements for a more sustainable and inclusive church polity strategy which is functional and practical. The question which is asked in this study is: how do church members perceive the competence of church leaders in interpretation of church orders, availability of trained church leaders in church polity, commitment of church policy makers, and competence of church members for implementation of church orders in Zambia?

Defining Terms

There have been great advances in academic discussion regarding the concept of church polity. I use the term church polity to refer to a multifaceted system of governance. It deals with issues of organization in the Church in relation to discipline and procedure and how the church relates to the state. In concrete terms, church polity is the sacred science of government for the visible church.

---

[1]   Pieter Coertzen, *Church and Order: A Reformed Perspective* (Leuven: Peeters, 1998), 53.

It studies the church order that applies and would apply in the church. In the same vein, it interprets general stipulations of the church order to ensure and promote things going well in church life.

The term church order refers to a collection of general stipulations, established by a competent, ecclesiastical entity and written down to ensure and promote good order in the life of the church. What is found in church polity must find its expression in the church order. The church order is a document that has binding character in a particular religious community, but also a document which intends to help the church live in an accountable way before God in all the facets of its existence.

The term church member, as often used in this article, expresses the idea of formal relationship between a local church and a Christian characterized by Christian's submission to the care of the church. In a broader sense, the term church member refers to Christians who have church membership with a particular denomination which includes both the church leaders and the congregation.

Within the Zambian context, the term 'church leader' is used and refers to both clergy and lay leaders. It should be noted that in the broader Zambian context this term further refers to the clergy.

The understanding of these terms and key concepts, in the article, is wider than it is normally envisioned to understand church polity. The intertwining of all societal dynamics are part of the framework. This conceptual understanding will be applied to this article.

Methodology

One hundred respondents (50 church leaders, thirty scholars and twenty church members) from five churches were selected from United Church of Zambia (UCZ), Anglican Church in Zambia (ACZ), Uniting Presbyterian Church in Southern Africa (UPCSA), Reformed Church in Zambia (RCZ|) and Church of Central Africa Presbyterian (CCAP) as well as from four theological institutions namely United Church of Zambia University (UCZU), Justo Mwale University (JMU), Evangelical University (EU) and St. John's Seminary. This study, therefore, relied on church orders, church leaders, and their church members as well as their differences in understanding of church polity, to describe the state of their perceptions of church orders at their churches.

The researcher's involvement in the ecumenical movement of Theological Education by Extension in Zambia (TEEZ) as member of the executive of the management leadership at national level from 2009-2013 came to know the polity and ecumenical involvement of the UCZ, ACZ, UPCSA, RCZ, and CCAP in fostering close links with other churches. As part of this research the polity of UCZ, ACZ, UPCSA, RCZ, and CCAP in Zambia, was done using literature study, the data collected were analyzed using the Norman Doe analysis[2] which includes an appendix which sets out fifty principles of law common to Christian churches. These express a basic theological truth and are drawn from the commonality of the regulatory systems found in different churches. However, these Christian laws vary from ordinary to the philosophical, from the theoretical to practical; they include aspects which are practical, theoretical, liturgical, and occasionally simply candid application of common sense.[3] Norman Doe's comparative study of principles of Christian laws gives focus and energy to the study of church polity.

Literature Review

Before giving details of the findings, the study will put them in context through a literature review of international and then Zambian-specific works. It is not possible to exhaust all literature for the global context, thus only a selection is used to demonstrate the current thinking and trends in church polity. The focus of this review is to highlight what happened in Zambia from the period 1995-2020.

The researcher has long recognized the necessity of devoting and mobilizing adequate resources, and of implementing appropriate church polity to benefit the church. A recent international conference highlighted several of the issues facing church polity, particularly Reformed church polity today.

---

[2]   This analysis looks at detailed comparative examination of judicial systems of churches in ten different global Christians. This analysis also looks at similarities between the contemporary regulatory instruments.

[3]   Norman Doe, *Christian Law: Contemporary Principles.*(Cambridge: Cambridge University Press, 2013), 388.

Mary-Anne Plaatjies van Huffel has argued the point that Reformed church polity principles have developed from being a concept related to church-state relationship to a concept that is essential to the governance of Reformed churches worldwide. She further advances the argument that the juridical character of Reformed church polity should be explained from a comprehensive viewpoint to highlight the various central values that Reformed churches share about the self-government of the church, the autonomy of the local congregation, and denominational ties. She finds that there is a uniformity of principles to which Reformed churches across the world agree. Again, she proposes that all Reformed churches should adhere to the minimum set of Reformed church governance principles.[4]

Practical Reformed church polity concerns and appreciation of new scholarly methods led Wim Dreyer to be dissatisfied with the quality of contemporary Reformed church order with the outdated available regulations. Drawing upon new strategies of church polity discoveries in the changing contexts, he proposes the need to create new church orders that would address the current problems within the Protestant churches.[5]

Church polity is theological science, argues Dries le Roy du Plooy, which must be rooted in Holy Scripture and the confession regarding the church providing guidelines for the church.[6] He further discusses the relationship between church polity and juridical science with a focus on the hermeneutics of church polity. He also suggests that much can be learned from the common law and from legal topics such as interpretation of legal text and documents. In addition, he asserts that if the hermeneutics of church

---

[4]   Mary-Anne Plaatjies van Huffel,"The Relevance of Reformed Church Polity Principles: Revisiting the Concept." In *Protestant Church Polity in Changing Contexts I: Ecclesiological and Historical Contributions, Proceedings of the International Conference, Utrecht, The Netherlands, 7-10 November 2011*, eds. Allan, J. Jansen & Leo, .J. Koffeman (Zürich: LIT Verlag, 2014), 45-46.

[5]   Wim Dreyer, "New Content, New Church Order," in *Protestant Church Polity in Changing Contexts II: Ecclesiological and Historical Contributions, Proceedings of the International Conference, Utrecht, The Netherlands, 7-10 November 2011*, eds. Leo .J. Koffeman & Johannes, Smit (Zürich: LIT Verlag, 2014),43.

[6]   Dries le Roy du Plooy, "The Foundation and Relevance of Reformed Church Polity as a Theological Science." in *Protestant Church Polity in Changing Contexts II: ecclesiological and Historical Contributions, Proceedings of the International Conference, Utrecht, The Netherlands, 7-10 November 2011*, eds. Leo J. Koffeman & Johannes Smit (Zürich: LIT Verlag, 2014), 5

polity were taken seriously in the church, little of the prevailing danger would exist in the church—both locally and ecumenically.[7]

In his comparative study of Episcopal, Presbyterian, and Congregational forms of governance, Leo Koffeman holds that each church system must be challenged theologically, and each includes challenges to the other systems, there is no ideal system—the only option is a truly ecumenical approach which recognizes that each church polity system is necessarily provisional,[8] and that church polity is there in order to serve the mission of the church.[9]

Koffeman suggests that the dialogue of theological and legal questions must open new possibilities to develop ecumenical church polity.[10] In this article, he seeks to address a new role of church polity in ecclesiology and ecumenism.

Barry Ensign-George and Hélène Evers argue that church polity can provide strategies for church unity, rather than just church division. This conclusion places ecumenism at the heart of the church and witness. The book also provides details on how church polity serves the missional nature of the church.[11]

Leepo Modise and Basimane Makoko suggest the development of church order will raise awareness of church unity.[12] One of the most important roles played by Modise and Makoko's work on church unity was to create and disseminate information about hindrances of church order to church unity through their research, what should be a realistic approach of church order for a visible church unity.[13]

Coertzen contends that, in the writing of church orders, the literature, such as works on natural law, positive law, the

---

[7] Du Plooy, "The Foundation and Relevance of Reformed Church Polity as a Theological Science," 17-18.

[8] Leo J. Koffeman, *In Order to Serve: An Ecumenical Introduction to Church Polity.* (Zürich: LIT Verlag, 2014), 61.

[9] Koffeman, *In Order to Serve,* 80.

[10] Leo J. Koffeman, "The Ecumenical Potential of Church Polity," *Ecclesiastical Law Journal 17, No. 2* (2015),193.

[11] Barry Ensign-George & Hélène Evers, *Church Polity, Mission and Unity: Their Impact in Church Life, Proceedings of the International Conference, Princeton, New Jersey, USA, 18-20 April 2016* (Zürich: LIT Verlag, 2019), 1-3.

[12] Leepo Modise & Basimane Makoko, "The Hindrances of Church Order to Church Union." In *Church Polity, Mission and Unity: Their Impact in Church Life, Proceedings of the International Conference,* Princeton, New Jersey, USA, 18-20 April 2016, eds. Barry, Ensign-George & Hélène, Evers (Zürich: LIT Verlag, 2019), 105.

[13] Modise & Makoko, "The Hindrances of Church Order to Church Union."105.

confession of faith, and other historical documents such as minutes and resolutions of church bodies should be consulted. At the same time the church fathers, who contributed to the philosophical and theological development of church polity, should also be consulted. When the church order has been formulated, it should be theologically accountable. And it should acknowledge that Jesus Christ is the head of the church.[14]

More specifically to Zambia, Gerdien Verstraelen-Gilhuis advocates making a new church order here because in the past there have been largely Zambian initiatives to develop better models for the handling of church matters.[15] She also points out the consequences of church union that, on the one hand, it produces new forms of Christianity and new expectations, but if is not well planned it may not be helpful to the church. Verstraelen-Gilhuis argues that the initiative of the RCZ to demand autonomy from the Dutch Reformed Church of South Africa also had a negative side because there were few trained personnel in the church.[16]

Historical study indicates that the church order that was formulated for the UCZ was one-sided: it concentrated on the organizational, rather than on the confessional side of the church. The main concern was to make a church order for maintaining order in, and the government of, the church.[17]

Analysis of UCZ, ACZ, RCZ, CCAP, and UPCSA[18]

[14]   Pieter Coertzen, *Decently and in Order: A Theological Reflection on the Order for, and Order in the Church*, 1st edn.(Leuven: Peeters, 2004),125-130.

[15]   Gerdien Verstraelen-Gilhuis, *From Dutch Mission Church to Reformed Church in Zambia: The Scope for African Leadership and Initiative in the History of a Zambian Mission Church* (Franeker: T Wever, 1982),336.

[16]   Verstraelen Gilhuis, *From Dutch Mission Church to Reformed Church of Zambia*, 336.

[17]   Peter, Bolink, *Towards Church Union in Zambia: A Study of Missionary Co-opera-tion and-Church Union Efforts in Central-Africa* (Franeker: T. Wever, 1967), 366-399.

[18]   *Table 1, 2 & 3 Juridical Analysis. ACZ. Constitution and Canons of the Church of Province of Central Africa*, Lusaka: ACZ, 1996, CCAP. Constitution, CCAP: Lusaka, 2010, RCZ. Constitution, by – Laws and Procedures, Lusaka: RCZ. 1965, RCZ. Constitution, by – Laws and Procedures, Lusaka: RCZ, 2010, UCZ. The Constitution on the Basis of Church union of UCZ, 1965, Kitwe: UCZ, 1965, UCZ. *Constitution, Rules and regulations*, Lusaka: UCZ, 1965, UCZ. Constitu-tion, *Rules and regulations*, Lusaka: UCZ, 1982, UCZ. *Constitution, Rules and regulations*, Lusaka: UCZ, 1984, UCZ. Constitution, Rules and regulations, Lusaka: UCZ, 1994, UCZ. *Constitution, Rules and regulations*, Lusaka: UCZ, 2004, UPCSA. *Manual of Faith and Order*, UPCSA: Johannesburg, 2007, UPCSA. Man-ual of Faith and Order, UPCSA: Johannesburg. 2010.

Themes	Unity	Doctrine	Church member-ship	Priesthood of all believers
UCZ	Article 3	Article 4	Article XI(4)	Article 8
ACZ	Canon 1 & 1a, Article V	Article V	Article 11, 12 & 13	Article 7
RCZ	Article 4(3)	Article 4	Article 6	Article 9, 18 & 19
CCAP	Article 14	Article 10	Article 17	Article 22
UPCSA	Chapter 2 Appendix E(1), E(2) & E(4)	Chapter 2:1-2:5	Chapter 1:3-5	Chapter 2.6.4, 2.6.5 & 2.6.6

Table 1

Themes	Church Discipline	Autonomy	Property	Laity
UCZ	Article 16	Article 17	Article 18	Article 9
ACZ	Canon 24, 25	Article 5	Canon 33	Article 7, Canon 14 & 18
RCZ	Article 4	Article 33	Article 33	Part IV
CCAP	Article 98	Article 28	Article 28	Article 99
UPCSA	Chapter 18	Chapter 12: 46-51	Chapter 12:69	Chapter 2.6.4, 2.6.5 & 2.6.6

Table 2

Themes	Baptism	Holy communion	Government of the church	Legal issues
UCZ	Article 5	Article 5	Article 11	Article 17
ACZ	Article 11	Article 14	Article 5	Article 5
RCZ	Article 3, BP 56: 1-6	Article 3, BP 56: 7-11	Article 5	Article 33
CCAP	Article 97	Article 97	Article 16	Article 95
UPCSA	Chapter 1:6-7 & Chapter 3	Chapter 1:6-7 & Chapter 4	Chapter 1:8-12	Chapter 12: 46-51

Table 3

This section begins with a brief survey of the selected legislative provisions of church orders of the UCZ, ACZ, RCZ, CCAP, and UPCSA, and then, after discussing the legislative provisions, more clearly relate that discussion to specific church polities. This juridical analysis shows the benefits of common legislative provisions of church orders. At the same time, it shows both good legislative provisions and the inadequate legislative provisions which are not working. It is important to identify whether these legislative provisions are strengthening unity or not.

It is clear from the tables that while the UCZ, CCAP, and UPCSA have the same roots in Scotland, they live differently in Zambia. This is because of the way the UCZ, CCAP, and UPCSA were established in Zambia by following the denominations of their missionary societies, for UCZ the church was established 1965 as result of church union of several churches which came together to form UCZ. While CCAP was established by CCAP from Malawi, and the UPCSA was established by Presbyterian Church Southern Africa (PCSA) from South Africa.[19]

The table shows that RCZ church order follows the Church Order of Dort very closely, except when it concerns the one who chairs the meeting it says the president. On the contrary, most African Presbyterian churches will prefer a Chair or Moderator to a President.

Table number 3 shows that UCZ, RCZ, CCAP, and UPCSA, the articles on Presbyterianism, discusses the reality that the power of the church is in the hands of the assemblies. Besides that, under the same article it notes that for a quorum to be constituted elders and ministers are required. However, I have a problem with this for a few reasons, especially that in CCAP and UPCSA there are deacons but they are not part of the quorum.

This study is faced with a methodological task in comparing church constitutions and theological education perspectives of the church polity of the church scholars, church leaders and church members with a view to determine the need for theological education of church polity.

---

[19] Godfrey Msiska, "Towards the Reconstruction of Church Polity in Zambia," in *Protestant Church Polity in Changing Contexts II: Ecclesiological and Historical Contributions, Proceedings of the International Conference, Utrecht, The Netherlands, 7-10 November 2011*, eds. Leo .J. Koffeman & Johannes, Smit, 111-129 (Zürich: LIT Verlag, 2014),122.

Respondents	Samples	Method	Demographic charac-teristic
Church leaders	50	Questionnaire	UCZ, ACZ, RCZ, CCAP, and UPCSA
scholars	30	Questionnaire	UCZ U, EU, JMU, and St. John's Seminary
Church members	20	Questionnaire	UCZ, ACZ, RCZ, CCAP, and UPCSA

Table 4.
Sample used in evaluation

Table 4 shows that a total number of 100 participants volunteered to take part in the research study. Of these, fifty were church leaders (both ministers (clergy) and lay leaders), 30 were scholars, and twenty were church members at UCZ, ACZ, RCZ, CCAP, and UPCSA. These included both males and females. Questionnaires were sent out by email, to the church leaders and as the number of responses above indicates, the response rate was very high. It is obvious that church leaders have significant interest in issues regarding church polity and ecumenism for them to attend to this. For scholars, completing a questionnaire may not just be a priority, and in the end thirty scholars participated in the study, both theologians and non-theologians at the UCZU, EU, JMU, and St. John's Seminary. Finally, twenty church members, both active and inactive, participated in the study.

Evaluation of the UCZ, ACZ, RCZ, CCAP, and UPCSA, during this period from 1995-2020, differences became clear and divisions among churches were most clear in the area of tribalism. RCZ among the Chewas, UPCSA in Zambia among the Tumbukas, Anglican among the Chewas, UCZ among the Bembas and Tongas and CCAP among the Tumbukas. In particular, two themes emerged. Ecclesial efforts to unify the churches which did not join the UCZ in 1965. And the second theme was the state efforts to unify the church in Zambia.

The results and recommendations of this research are to be made available more widely than to just the participants and scholars, although the participants and scholars would have priority access. Theological colleges and ecumenical institutions and churches would also greatly benefit from this study especially that it has emerged from the context of Zambia. Generally, this study is for all those who are involved in theology and religious studies. It is my wish that this study will encourage those who are involved in ecumenism, church polity, church history, and theology.

Apart from that, the responses from scholars on church polity should be viewed as church policies. Church policies as a common-sense guide for administering churches and for safeguarding the well-being for all the members of the churches Church policies which makes all Christians welcomed, respected, and safe in their churches.

First, a few preliminary observations and reflections. It is clear from the responses that the challenge for most theological faculties

Themes	Scholars from UCZU, EU, JMU, and St. John's Seminary Yes or No	Church leaders from UCZ, ACZ, RCZ, CCAP and UPCSA Yes or No	Church members from UCZ, ACZ, RCZ, CCAP and UPCSA Yes or No
Competence of church leaders in interpretation of church orders	20 said yes 10 said no	40 said yes 10 said no	5 said yes 15 said no
Availability of trained church leaders in church polity	5 said yes 25 said no	5 said yes 45 said no	15 said yes 5 said no
Commitment of church policy makers	10 said yes 20 said no	40 said yes 10 said no	5 said yes 15 said no
Competence of church members for implementation of church orders	5 said yes 25 said no	10 said yes 40 said no	5 said yes 15 said no

Table 5

is that they focus more on scholarly achievement and technicalities of church polity rather than church polity 'multilingualism' in spite of the fact that church polity is ecumenical in nature. But most theological institutions ignore this very important area of multilingualism. In fact, most of these interdenominational theological institutions are, therefore, not appreciated. In my view, Christians should learn from one another so that no one monopolizes the true faith or practices better than the other. The church should be forever one rather than divided.

From the responses of scholars, it is clear that theological students graduating from the same theological institutions have a common shared theological training at one place with same theological identity but when sent to serve in a congregation each student identifies with their denomination regardless of whether it is the UCZ, ACZ, RCZ, CCAP, and PCSA.

Competence of Church Leaders In Interpretation of Church Orders

The results in tables 4 and 5 for competence of church leaders in interpretation of church orders indicated that three broad areas were considered for the study. Each area was measured using four items. These results showed that scholars and church leaders agree that church leaders are competent in the interpretation of church orders. Although of the church members surveyed, five said that church leaders were competent and fifteen said that they were not competent.

However, lack of theological training in church polity for church leaders in both churches and theological institutions is a serious problem that stands in the way of successful interpretation of church orders. Rian Venter affirms that the importance of church polity is an academic challenge in that Church polity should reflect the exigencies of the African reality; this is a task still to be addressed in Zambia.[20] Evidence of lack of competence of church leaders in the interpretation of church orders shows there is a need for well-trained and qualified church leaders in both churches and theological institutions to teach church polity to church members.

---

[20]　Rian Venter,"Theological Education for a New Millennium, Zambia Justo Mwale Theological College: A Story of Theological Education in Zambia towards the Third Millennium," *Theological Forum REC*, 27, No. 5, (October 1999): 3.

Availability of Trained Church Leaders in Church Polity

The second item on the table is the availability of trained church leaders in church polity. The results showed that very few church leaders have been trained in church polity. Both scholars and church leaders disagree as to the availability of trained church leaders in church polity. On the other hand, church members agreed that their churches have the availability of trained church leaders in church polity. This is because church members assume that their church leaders are well-trained because they occupy leadership positions. On the other hand, church scholars and church leaders disagree because some of the scholars are also church leaders. The church scholars who are also church leaders are familiar with church polity and church practices. Mulenga Chilekwa observes that UCZ has been a passive recipient of much of its missionary inheritance and has lacked the confidence to revisit its received beliefs and practices.[21]

Commitment of Church Policy Makers

In the question of the commitment of church policy makers, the result showed that, within the church, the church policy makers were perceived as quite committed to implementing functional church policies in their churches. The result showed that church leaders and church members agree that church policy makers were quite serious about church members acquiring knowledge of church policies. While the scholars disagree on the commitment of church policy makers to some extent, because of the fact that some of the scholars are also church leaders as well, and so the church scholars who are also church leaders are familiar with church polity and church practices.

The commitment of church policy makers is demonstrated by their commitment to includes these selected articles, canons and regulations in their church orders and church constitutions: church government and unity, doctrine, church membership, priesthood of all believers and the laity, autonomy and legal issues, property, church discipline, baptism, and holy communion.Church

---

[21]   Mulenga, Chilekwa,"The United Church of Zambia 1965- 1995: A Critical Exploration of History, Faith and Practice of United Church, with Suggestions for the Future Agenda." Master's Thesis, School of Humanities. (Oxford: Westminster College, 1998), 93.

Government and Unity

Both table 3 and table 1 shows that the four church orders of UCZ, RCZ, CCAP, and UPCSA have shared historical development of Presbyterian Church government and follow presbyterial principles In particular, are the principles of the rule by plurality of elders in the local congregation, the principle of submission of a local governing body to a broader governing body, and the unity of church finding its most concrete representation in connection of churches and their elders in regional and trans-regional bodies. In that case, I want to argue that the last point on unity is a good principle but most of the Presbyterian family are not connected to each other as a denomination. From the table, ACZ church government shows that it is governed by bishops, while UCZ, RCZ, CCAP, and the UPCSA hold to governance by elders who are spiritually mature.

Doctrine

Article V of the constitution of the ACZ clearly asserts that the episcopal synod which consists only of bishops of the province who have final authority in matters concerning preservation of the truth of the church's doctrine, purity of life, and worthiness of worship. Synods have very wide authority to legislate, but the authority of bishops on matters of faith and order is final.

From the legislative provisions the UCZ, ACZ, RCZ, CCAP, and UPCSA, believe that the Bible is the Word of God and that the Holy Spirit makes Holy Scripture the Word of God, the message in which God reveals himself and gives himself to humans. The church is a living body within which the proper interpretation of Scripture is kept alive.[22]

Church Membership

The model of a membership roll is inherited from missionaries. What are the implications of the missionary inherited model of church membership to traditional understanding of membership? Today, church members are not interested in the model of a membership roll. They want a church with open doors–not a legally binding prescriptive list.

[22]   Alister E. McGrath, 2011, *The Christian Theology Reader*, 4th ed. (Chechester: Wiley-Blackwell Publishers), 409.

Autonomy and Legal Issues

From tables 2 and 3, it is possible to see the place of autonomy in the legislative provisions of these five churches. However the discussion on the autonomy of the UPCSA in Zambia from the UPCSA has been focusing on Venn's three –'selves': self-governing, self-propagating, and self-sustaining.[23] The main problem identified in the UPCSA Synod of Zambia strategic plan 2007-2009 on the weaknesses was that UPCSA in Zambia has no legislative power.[24] It is worth noting that the UCZ, ACZ, RCZ, and CCAP have legislative powers on matters of faith and order, but UPCSA in Zambia has no legislative power.

Property

From ecclesiastical jurisprudence, one can see that the highest council has control of the ownership of land and consequent responsibilities. Such interests could be mortgages, leases, licenses, easements, or profits. All these are responsibilities of the highest council to deal with: rights and liabilities of landowners or property owners. In the case of the UPCSA the ownership of land and their interest is held in the hands of a presbytery. Between all the churches, it is true that legal ownership rights are with the highest council who have the right to use, to possess, and to manage the property.

Church Discipline

In evaluating church discipline within the ranks of the UCZ, ACZ, RCZ, CCAP, and UPCSA, it is important to give a brief historical development of ecclesiastical discipline. It should be said that church discipline has developed through different contexts and with different applications influenced by different political and ecclesiastical situations. The question is how church discipline can reflect the exigency of Zambian reality? Of course, the immediate answer to this question is through contextualization.

Church discipline has developed as a result of different historical and contextual situations. For that reason, it is very

---

[23]   Gerald, H. Anderson, *Biographical Dictionary for Christian Missions* (Grand Rapids, Ml: Eerdmans.1999), 698.

[24]   UPCSA. *Synod of Zambia Strategic Plan for 2007-2009* (Lusaka: UPCSA Synod of Zambia, 2007), 3-4.

important to note that there are many Reformers who contributed to the development of church discipline. Along with that, church discipline aims at maintaining the purity of the church which is the Body of Christ. This, then, is the other point that has affected efforts at church unity in Zambia. In 2001, RCZ excommunicated eight ministers; however, some of the church members from the RCZ followed the excommunicated ministers affecting the church unity in the RCZ.[25]

Baptism and Holy Communion

Evaluating the UCZ, ACZ, RCZ, CCAP, and UPCSA views on Baptism and Holy Communion, it is clear that these churches in Zambia can achieve the visible unity they seek as one of the essential prerequisites is that they should be in basic agreement on the sacraments. From the legislative provisions on Baptism and Holy Communion, therefore, these churches are already in agreement. However, as much as there is wide agreement, in terms of order, on Baptism and Holy Communion, I get an impression that these churches do not agree on understanding of interpretation of Scripture regarding Baptism and Holy Communion.

On the aspect of commitment of church policy makers, these selected themes from their church orders of UCZ, ACZ, RCZ, CCAP, and UPCSA, shows that church policy makers are committed. There is no doubt that church policy makers are committed to the type of church orders they now have. These church orders are regulations that value order and rules in the churches more than new experiences—meaning renewal of some church positions—and these are inherited church orders from the colonial church orders of church polity left by European missionaries.

Competence of Church Members for Implementation of Church Orders

The results under competence of church members for implementation of church orders showed that scholars, church leaders, and church members disagree about church members not being eager to implement church orders.

---

[25]   Godfrey, Msiska, "Towards the Reconstruction of Church Polity in Zambia." 115.

The implication of these findings and the supporting evidence from this study is that there is a need for theological education in church polity in Zambia in order to overcome the challenges posed by church members not eager to implement church orders. On the other hand, there is also a need for more theological education in church polity for church leaders.

Towards a More Sustainable and Inclusive Church Polity Strategy

After comparing constitutions of UCZ, PCSA, RCZ, ACZ, and CCAP, it seems to me that their constitutions need to be reviewed and brought up to date to allow the laity to have greater part in the 'running of the church,' and the Reformed teaching of the priesthood of all believers should be taken seriously. Peter Tie makes it clear that:

> The doctrine of priesthood of all believers was partially retained by the early church fathers, clearly restricted by Cyprians, virtually repressed in middle ages, definitely rediscovered by the early reformers, consequently reinterpreted by later Protestants and eventually restored.[26]

I am of the opinion that priesthood of all believers is essentially significant and applicable in the Protestant churches in Zambia. Johnson holds that:

> The priesthood of all believers implies the spiritual equality of all Christians before God. This meant that the leadership of the church was shared by the whole community. No single person or office was given power to carry out discipline or exercise the rights of church governance.[27]

The priesthood of all believers means it is the corporate responsibility of all believers to discern and determine the will of God under the Lordship of Christ and leading of the Holy Spirit as they serve God in communities to encourage participation of all Christians in

[26]   Peter L. Tie, *Restore Unity, Recover Identity and Refine Orthopraxy: The believers Priesthood in the Ecclesiology of James Leo Garrett Jr.* (Eugene, Oregon: Wipf and Stock Publishers, 2012), 16.

[27]   William. Stacy, Johnson, *John Calvin, Reformer for the 21st Century* (Louisville: Westminster John Knox Press, 2009),89.

evangelization, communal fellowship, mutual servanthood, and congregational participation.

Here Johnson cites John Calvin who said that all believers in the church are considered equal in the eyes of God. In describing Calvin's understanding of the priesthood of all believers, Johnson notes that '"Calvin did not even use the term laity, for he did not want to hint at any difference in rank between pastor and the rest of church membership."[28]

The lay training should be understood in terms of equipping the laity to live and act as leaven in the world and society. This can be understood from the meeting of the third Assembly of the World Council of Churches in New Delhi in 1961 which described Christian people as "a letter from Christ to the world":

> We Christian people, wherever we are, are a letter from Christ to his world, written not with ink with the Spirit of the living God, not on tablets of stone but on tablets of human hearts. The message is that God in Christ has reconciled the world to himself. Let us speak and live it with joy and confidence, for it is to give the light of the knowledge of the glory of God in the face of Jesus Christ.[29]

The emphasis of this meeting was on both participation of clergy and laity in the life of the church. At the 1948 Amsterdam Assembly of the World Council of Churches, the Assembly reported that:

> The laity constitutes more than ninety-nine percent of the church...only the witness of a spiritually intelligent and active laity can the church meet the modern world in its actual perplexities and life situations. We need to rethink what it means to speak of the church as a royal priesthood, holy nation, a peculiar people, and Body of Christ to which every member constitutes in his measure.[30]

It appears that the majority of Christians that constitute the letter from Christ to the world are lay people whose witness comes

---

[28]   Johnson, *John Calvin, Reformer for the 21st Century*, 90.

[29]   Willem Adoph, Visser't Hooft, "New Delhi Speaks About Christian Witness, Service and Unity." (*The message, Appeal and section Reports of the Third Assembly of World Council of Churches*, Held in New Delhi, India, November 11to December 1961). (New York: Association Press, 1962), 20.

[30]   Visser't Hooft, "New Delhi Speaks About Christian Witness, Service and Unity."153-154.

through their daily lives, work, relationships with one another, within the human communities, and whenever they may be in God's world.

This research observes that the ministry of the church in Zambia reveals that an unacceptably large amount of time, resources and energy are spent on ministerial formation, and this is in spite of the fact that within the Protestant churches in Zambia, that laity plays a crucial role in the life of churches.

Conclusion

The article has examined the comparisons and contrasts of various church constitutions and their developments in the identified areas. At the same time, this article has shown the need for more theological education in church polity in Zambia.

www.ingramcontent.com/pod-product-compliance
Lightning Source LLC
LaVergne TN
LVHW021543080426
835509LV00019B/2810